Light Action!

ACTION!

AMAZING EXPERIMENTS WITH OPTICS

Vicki Cobb and Josh Cobb

ILLUSTRATED BY THEO COBB

HarperCollinsPublishers

All the experiments in this book have been tested and are safe. However, misuse of materials, failure to follow the specified procedure, failure to heed cautions, and carelessness can result in injury. Each experiment should be read in its entirety so that the reader is fully aware of any safety notices and cautions before performing it.

A child using this book should check with a parent or guardian before attempting any experiment. Adult participation is encouraged for enlightenment as well as for safety.

The publisher cannot be responsible for any difficulties, including injury, that result from failure of the reader to carry out the experiments properly, failure to heed safety notices and cautions, or failure to supervise a youngster carrying out the experiments.

Library of Congress Cataloging-in-Publication Data
Cobb, Vicki.
    Light action! : amazing experiments with optics / by Vicki Cobb and Josh Cobb ; illustrated by Theo Cobb.
        p.   cm.
    Summary: Explains what light is and explores the basic principles of optics through experiments.
        ISBN 0-06-021436-8. — ISBN 0-06-021437-6 (lib. bdg.)
    1. Optics—Juvenile literature.   2. Light—Experiments—Juvenile literature.   [1. Optics. 2. Light.]   I. Cobb, Josh.   II. Cobb, Theo, ill.   III. Title.
QC360.C6   1993   92-22528
535'.078—dc20   CIP
                                                       AC

For Abigail Jane Cobb

The authors gratefully acknowledge the critical contributions of Doug Goodman, Ph.D., and Candace Flattery-Freedenberg, but accept full responsibility for the accuracy of the text.

ALSO BY VICKI COBB

MAGIC . . . NATURALLY!:
SCIENCE ENTERTAINMENTS AND AMUSEMENTS

CHEMICALLY ACTIVE: EXPERIMENTS
YOU CAN DO AT HOME

THE SECRET LIFE OF COSMETICS: A SCIENCE
EXPERIMENT BOOK

THE SECRET LIFE OF HARDWARE: A SCIENCE
EXPERIMENT BOOK

THE SECRET LIFE OF SCHOOL SUPPLIES

HOW TO *REALLY* FOOL YOURSELF: ILLUSIONS
FOR ALL YOUR SENSES

MORE SCIENCE EXPERIMENTS YOU CAN EAT

SCIENCE EXPERIMENTS YOU CAN EAT

Contents

One **SHEDDING LIGHT ON LIGHT**   1

Two **BLOCKING LIGHT**   9
The Anatomy of a Shadow   10
Making Shadows   14
Thinking of Light as a Stream of Particles   19
Translucency   19
Make a Dark Spot White   20

Three **BENDING LIGHT**   25
Make Money Appear Before Your Eyes   28
Thinking of Light as Waves   29
False Pencils in Water   33
Hot-Air Mirages . . . Without a Desert!   37
Lose a Glass in a Glass   38

Four **LIGHT BENDERS**   43
A Light Bender in Action   48
Watch TV Upside Down on a Piece of Paper   51
A Rear-Projection Projector   54
The Swimming-Pool Effect   56
An Ice Lens   57
Grinding an Ice Lens   60

Five **BOUNCING LIGHT**   63
Turn On Your TV from Another Room   64
Off-the-Wall TV Control   67
Watch TV with a Curved Mirror   69
Make a Big-Screen TV with a Curved Mirror   71
See the Astigmatism in a Curved Mirror   72

Six GUIDING LIGHT   79
   Send Light Through a Glass Baking Dish   80
   Make a Coin Disappear in a Bowl of Water   86
   Wipe Away the Image of a Coin with Your Hand   88
   Transparent Gelatin that Light Cannot
      Get Through   90
   Pouring Light   92

Seven BREAKING UP LIGHT   97
   A Water Prism   98
   Colored Lights Through Water   100
   Make a Rainbow in Your Backyard   102
   Make a Sunset in a Glass of Water   103

Eight COLOR   109
   Make a Green Gumball Black   110
   Mixing Light   112
   Color Wheel   115
   Color Television and Color Print   117
   Clear Glass that Light Cannot Get Through   120
   "Whiter than White" Soap   121
   Lasers   123
   Unseen Colors   125

Nine MAKING WAVES   129
   The Ripple Tank   130
   Diffraction Between Wax Blocks   133
   Interference in a Ripple Tank   135
   Bubble Films   138
   Oil Slicks   141
   Colors in Clear Acetate   141
   A Pocket Comb with False Teeth   142

Feather Fringes 144
Colorful Compact Discs 145
Holograms 146

Ten **POLARIZED LIGHT** 153
The Moving Rope and the Gate 153
A Glare Hunt 156
Block Light with a Piece of Transparent Tape 157
Make a Rainbow Appear and Disappear 160
Sunglasses that Stop Time 163
Stressed-Out Gelatin 164
Hunting for Stress 165
The Depolarizer 167
Light-Flopping Syrup 167

Eleven **CATCHING LIGHT** 173
Make a Ghost Appear on a Wall 175
The Blind Spot 177
Catch Light on a Silver Tray 180
Searching for Electric Eyes 182
Fool a Doorbell 184
Photosynthesis 186
The Light that Makes Food 187
Light and the Energy Crisis 191
Index 193

Chapter One

SHEDDING LIGHT ON LIGHT

If the human race had been born blind, everything that we know about our surroundings would have had to be discovered through touching, smelling, tasting, and hearing. However, our eyes detect light. Light has been a source of information about our immediate world and has added immeasurably to our understanding of it. In addition, light has been our main source of information about the sun, planets, stars, and other heavenly bodies. Only the moon has been explored directly, and that's been in recent times. It is very human to wonder about things—like the universe—that are bigger than ourselves. It is also human to wonder about the nature of light, which brings the universe to us.

Vision, our ability to detect light, is the most dominant of our five senses. One measure of this is that we have more receptor cells in our eyes to detect light than we have receptor cells for all our other senses combined. Another is the enormous range of things we perceive, including brightness, color, contrast, depth, and motion. We are aware of light every conscious moment of our lives. So it is no surprise that many people have spent time thinking about the nature of light.

Some ideas about light go back thousands of years. In the first century A.D., a Greek engineer named Hero (20?A.D.–?) wrote a book about mirrors and light. He believed that light was a kind of "feeler" or antenna sent out by the eyes to detect the things we saw. Hero thought that light traveled infinitely fast.

About nine hundred years later, an Arabian physicist named Alhazen (965?–1039) figured out that light comes from a source, such as the sun, and that everything we see reflects light from the source to our eyes. Alhazen wrote a book about light that was translated into Latin in the thirteenth century, three hundred years after he wrote it. It had a powerful influence on scientists who studied light.

Two theories arose about the nature of light. One theory said that light was a stream of particles that traveled in straight lines. The other said that light was made of waves. Evidence for both ideas came as scientists observed the behavior of light in their laboratories and in nature. Through experimentation they found that light can be blocked, bent, bounced, broken up, caught, filtered, and scattered. Everything we do with light reveals something about its nature. All the information we have collected about light is called the science of *optics*. The word "optics" comes from a Greek word (*optikos*) meaning "of the eye or seeing."

Any study of light begins with a source of light. The most obvious and most important source of light is the sun. Through the ages we have created other sources of light to be able to go about our business when sunlight was not available. First, there was light produced by fire. Candles and oil, and then gas lamps, illuminated people's homes for centuries. In 1879, Thomas Edison (1847–1931) introduced the first incandescent electrical lamp. An incandescent lamp uses a wire thread that is heated by an electric current until it glows. Other forms of electrical light sources are arc lamps, in which the light is a series of bright sparks, and fluorescent lamps.

The science of optics has given us the power to do some amazing things: Grocery checkout devices use a scanning laser beam to identify an item by its code, made of black bars; the checkout device then displays the price of the item on a screen. Compact disc players also use lasers to read music that has been encoded on special optical discs. Credit cards now have holograms,

which are pictures with a three-dimensional appearance. Holograms are made using lasers. They are so hard to copy that they make it difficult for criminals to counterfeit credit cards. Photocopiers and fax machines use light to reproduce printed material in seconds. Light, passing through fiber-optic cables, can carry telephone calls over thousands of miles or let us peer directly inside the human body without cutting it open. We become couch potatoes as we use a form of light to change channels on our TVs without getting up. Learning about the properties of light has enabled us to see in the dark, to see through solid material, to see objects too tiny or too far away for the human eye. Light certainly will be an essential part of many great technological breakthroughs in the future.

You can experience the wonders of optics for yourself. This book shows you how. Before you begin, let us give you a few suggestions about how to use this book.

You can simply read this book from cover to cover as you would any book. Optics is presented here in a logical fashion, chapter by chapter, each topic building on ideas introduced earlier. Light is not a simple subject. For this reason, it is better not to skip around while reading this book.

The important ideas in each chapter are illustrated by experiments, which are the heart of a science like optics. The best way to use this book is to do the experiments in order as you read along.

When you do an experiment, read through the *procedure* and collect everything you need before you start. The procedure is the step-by-step way a scientist goes about getting information. Good procedures give clear-cut results. They also suggest other procedures for further experimentation. If you get ideas for other experiments while doing our procedures (and you probably will), keep on going. We have tried all the procedures in this book in our home laboratory and they work. But you may think of ways to improve them. Go to it! Science is the most fun when you make discoveries of your own.

Optics is an adventure worth getting your head and hands into. Once you do, the world will never look the same again. That's a promise!

Chapter 2

·

BLOCKING LIGHT

When light is blocked, a shadow is created. So what else is new? Shadows are so common that most people never stop to think about them. But shadows reveal some fascinating properties of light. Go on a shadow hunt around your house. See if you can find examples of these kinds of shadows: darker shadows and lighter shadows and shadows with both light and dark parts; shadows with crisp outlines and shadows with fuzzy outlines and shadows that have no outlines; shadows that are larger than the object that casts them and shadows that are smaller; and multiple shadows cast by the same object. Suddenly shadows don't seem quite as simple as they may have appeared at first glance. One way to begin understanding shadows is to make them, as you'll see in the first two experiments.

THE ANATOMY OF A SHADOW

Materials & Equipment

- a large desk lamp with a flexible neck that can be put in a variety of positions
- a white wall or screen
- a pencil
- aluminum foil
- a magnifying glass

Procedure #1

Cover the opening of the lampshade with the aluminum foil so that no light gets out and place the lamp as far from the wall or screen as you can. Poke a half-inch to one-inch hole in the center of the foil with the pencil so that light escapes from the lamp. Point this light toward the wall. This light will be your light source for shadow making. Next, remove all other light sources. Close the curtains or blinds and make the room as dark as possible. Turn off any other lamps in the room. The room will be only dimly illuminated.

Hold your hand a few inches away from the wall and examine the shadow it casts. Notice how sharp and well defined the edges of the shadow are. Now step back from the wall toward the lamp and see how the shadow changes. What happens to its size? What happens to the crispness of its edges? See two parts of a shadow emerge as you move. The darkest part of the shadow is called the *umbra*. The lighter area that surrounds the umbra is called the *penumbra*.

Be aware that the lamp can get hot. Be sure to

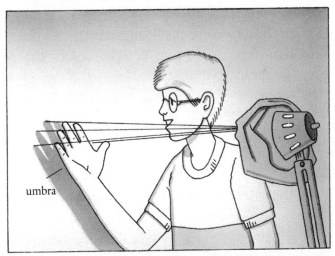

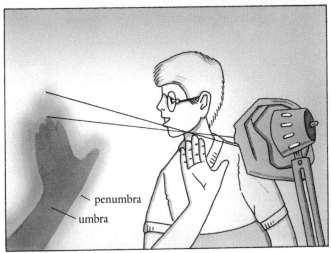

turn off the lamp and remove the foil when you are finished.

Here's What's Happening

An *opaque* object, in this case your hand, blocks all the light that hits it and casts a shadow on the wall opposite the light source. Light that gets past the edges of an opaque object strikes the surface surrounding the shadow. When your hand is close to the wall, the outline of its shadow is crisp, and the penumbra is so small that you might have to use a magnifying glass to see it (something you might want to try). The crispness of your shadow demonstrates a very important property of light: Light travels in straight lines.

The light source in this experiment was small, but it still had a size. All light sources of any appreciable size produce light that *spreads* from the source in straight lines in all directions at every conceivable angle. Whether or not a particular light ray is blocked depends on its angle when it reaches the boundary of an opaque object. A single point on the edge of your hand was struck by rays originating from every point of the light source (from every point in the hole in the aluminum foil). A ray of light from one side of the light source may not be blocked by the edge of your hand, while a ray from another part is blocked. The umbra is the area of a shadow where all the light rays are blocked. If all the rays came as parallel lines, there would only be an umbra. But they don't. They come at many angles, crisscrossing each other. The penumbra is the area where only some of the rays are blocked and other rays pass.

When your hand is close to the wall, the distance between your hand and the wall is too short for the rays to spread very much. The outline of the umbra is so close to the outline of the penumbra that it's almost impossible to detect. The shadow is crisp. When your hand moves farther from the wall, the rays have more room to spread out, increasing the sizes of both the umbra and the penumbra. As the size of the penumbra increases, the outlines of the shadow become fuzzier.

As your hand gets closer to the light source, it blocks more of the light, and the shadow gets larger.

Procedure #2

You can increase the size of the light source by removing the aluminum foil from the lamp. The difference in the shadow cast by your hand can be shown more dramatically if you hold your hand about a foot from the wall and then have a friend remove the foil. What happens to the sizes of the penumbra and umbra when you increase the size of the light source?

Here's What's Happening

Increasing the size of the light source increases the number of light rays. It also increases the range of angles of the light rays that hit your hand. More rays get around your hand, so the size of the penumbra increases. The umbra gets smaller because outside rays from the larger light source strike places that were inside the original umbra.

There are four main *variables* (things that can change) that affect a shadow. These variables are: the size and shape of the object casting the shadow, the size and shape of the light source, the distance from the object to the shadow, and the distance from the object to the light source.

MAKING SHADOWS

Here are some fun activities you can do with shadows. See if you can figure out which variables you are changing.

Hand Shadows

Use a single source of light in a darkened room. You can hold your hands in different positions to create silhouettes of different creatures on the wall. With practice, you can make the jaws of the fox open and close, the trunk of the elephant swing, and the ears of the rabbit and the wings of the bird move.

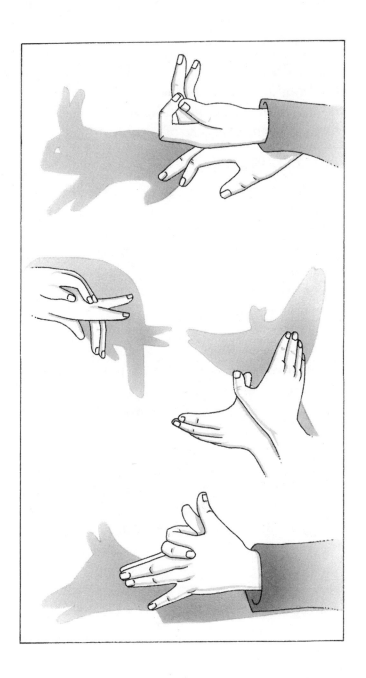

Cast a Giant Shadow

In a darkened room, place a light source near the floor at one end of the room. Stand in front of the light. Experiment by moving back and forth to change the size of your shadow.

Shadow Portraits

You can use shadows to draw true-to-life silhouettes of your friends and family. Use a small light source and tape a piece of paper to the wall. Have a friend stand near the wall so his or her face casts a profile shadow on the paper. Trace the profile on the paper. With practice, you can get very good likenesses.

Double Shadows

Use two sources of light that have identical light bulbs and are separated from each other. Experiment with different lamp positions. If you use your hand as the object, try varying its distance from the light sources and the wall. Put the two lamps close together. Move your hand closer and closer to the wall. See what happens to the separation of the shadows.

When the two lamps are next to each other, the two shadows are also quite close together. The umbra is where both shadows overlap. The penumbra has a distinct outline. This is a more dramatic example of Procedure #1.

Eclipses

An eclipse of the moon occurs when the earth moves between the sun and the moon. The curved shadow of the earth can be seen as it moves across the face of a full moon. When you see a lunar eclipse, you really are seeing only the

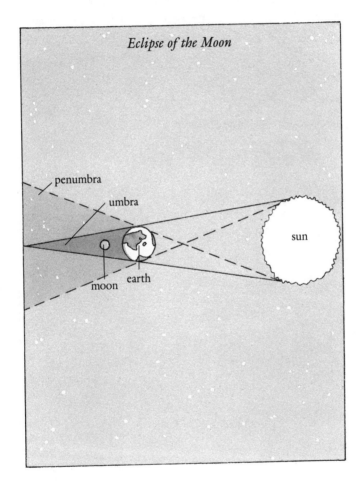

Eclipse of the Moon

umbra of the earth's shadow. The penumbra is so light that it's hardly noticeable.

An eclipse of the sun is the moon's shadow falling on the earth as the moon passes between the sun and the earth. Since the moon is smaller than the earth, its shadow produces both an umbra and a penumbra on earth. The area of the earth shadowed by the umbra is the area considered to be in total solar eclipse. The area shadowed by the penumbra is said to be in partial solar eclipse.

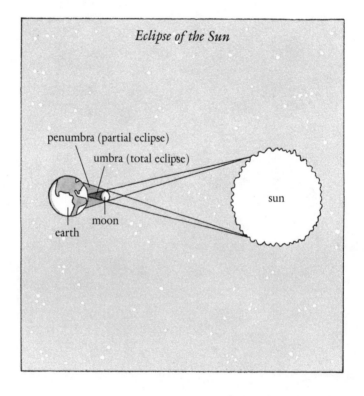

Eclipse of the Sun

penumbra (partial eclipse)

umbra (total eclipse)

sun

moon

earth

As the moon covers the sun, darkness descends. In the area of total eclipse, it gets about as dark as twilight. In the partially eclipsed areas, the sky darkens but you can see a crescent sun, and it still appears to be daylight.

THINKING OF LIGHT AS A STREAM OF PARTICLES

The way light behaves gave people ideas about the nature of light. The formation of shadows led them to think that light rays are streams of tiny particles. After all, when particles of flour from a sifter fall on an object, a "flour shadow" forms underneath the object. The idea that light is made of particles can explain the formation of shadows, but scientists soon discovered that this idea could not explain other light phenomena, as you'll discover later.

TRANSLUCENCY

Unlike *opaque* objects, *translucent* materials only partially block light. Some light passes through them; however, not enough passes through to let us see a clear image like the ones we see through a *transparent* object such as window glass. Some materials are more translucent than others, and some materials can be made to be more translucent. Look around for translucent things. Here are some examples you might find: paper, some plastics, window shades, glass bricks, bathroom windows, shower curtains, and lampshades.

The next experiment will show you how to change the translucency of a piece of paper.

MAKE A DARK SPOT WHITE

Materials & Equipment
- a piece of white typing paper
- salad oil
- a paper towel
- a bright lamp

Procedure
Put a drop of oil on the paper to make a spot. Wipe off the excess oil with the paper towel. Shine the lamp onto the paper and notice that the oil spot looks darker than the surrounding white paper. Now hold the paper up between you and the lamp. Which is darker now, the oil spot or the paper?

Here's What's Happening
The way light passes through paper is somewhat complicated. Paper is a matted sheet of tiny cellulose fibers. Cellulose is the structural material of all plants, and its fibers are transparent. Air is present among the matted fibers in a piece of paper. Although both are transparent, the combi-

nation of clumps of fibers and pockets of air produces a material that most light cannot travel through in a straight line. The paper is more opaque than translucent.

When the air spaces are filled with oil or wax, the light has a more uniform (and therefore easier) material to pass through. When you shine light on your side of the white paper, some of the light passes through the paper, but most of the light is reflected back to your eyes. In the area where the oil is, more light passes through the paper. As a result, the oil spot appears darker than the rest of the paper. When you hold the paper up to the lamp and look toward the light through the paper, the added light passing through the oil makes that spot look whiter than the surrounding paper, which is blocking most of the light.

Early settlers of this country often covered the windows of their log cabins with oiled paper until they could afford to replace it with glass. The oiled paper kept out the cold but allowed the light to come through.

Tracing paper is more translucent than typing paper because the fibers are packed more closely together, making a more uniform material with fewer air spaces to interfere with the transmission of light. You can use a sheet of tracing paper as a screen for shadows. Find a way to suspend a piece of tracing paper at least a foot from a lamp.

Place your hands between the lamp and the paper to cast your hand shadows on the back of the paper. View the shadows from the other side. This kind of translucent screen lets others see the figures created by your shadows without your hands getting in the way.

Chapter Three

BENDING LIGHT

Shadows are evidence that light travels in straight lines. Because light travels in straight lines, you can't see around corners. But light can be bent, as you'll see in the next two chapters. The bending of light depends on another property of light—namely, its speed. Measuring the speed of light is one of the great breakthroughs of science.

You see a flash of lightning and you hear its thunder seconds later. You see a batter swing at a baseball from your seat high in the stands and, after a noticeable pause, you hear the crack of the bat. These observations lead to the conclusion that it takes sound longer to reach your ears than it takes light to reach your eyes. Clearly, sound takes time to travel. The question is, how fast does light travel? If light does take time to travel from one place to another, it must move so fast that its speed seems impossible to measure. The ancient Greek engineer Hero believed the speed of light to be infinitely fast. This means that you should be able see light simultaneously at the beginning and end of its journey, but that doesn't make sense. So about sixteen hundred years after Hero, scientists began to tackle the enormous task of determining the speed of light.

One of the first scientists to make an attempt was the Italian astronomer and physicist Galileo Galilei (1564–1642). He took a lantern to the top of one hill while his assistant took a lantern to the top of another. Galileo opened the shutter on his own lantern. The assistant opened the shutter on his lantern as soon as he saw Galileo's light. Galileo knew the distance between the two hilltops. He hoped that he could measure the time interval between the opening of his lantern and the appearance of the assistant's light. If he knew the distance and the time, he could calculate the speed. Galileo made many measurements between different pairs of hills. But his measurement of time was very inaccurate. All he really measured was how long it took his partner to react to his light and for him to react to his partner's light. The speed of light proved to be much too fast to be measured in this crude manner.

The first reasonable estimate of the speed of

light was made by the Danish astronomer Olaus Roemer (1644–1710) in 1676. Roemer carefully watched the moons of Jupiter. The moon closest to Jupiter was eclipsed every time it rotated behind the planet. Roemer discovered that the time between eclipses was shorter when the earth was moving toward Jupiter and was longer when the earth was moving away from Jupiter. Roemer correctly figured that the eclipses actually occurred at regular intervals, but that when he saw them depended on when the light reached him. When the earth was moving toward Jupiter, it took less time for the light to travel the millions of miles to earth than when the earth was moving away. Roemer's calculation for the speed of light was based on when he figured he should see the eclipse, when he actually saw it, and the extra distance the light had to travel to reach the earth. He figured the speed of light to be 140,000 miles per second, which was 20 percent too slow—not bad for a first try.

Other scientists developed more accurate ways to measure the speed of light. Albert Michelson (1852–1931), a German-born American physicist, spent forty years of his life at this task. His measurements, which he made with American chemist Edward Morley (1838–1923), made scientific history and were a factor in earning him a Nobel Prize in 1907. Their ingenious experiments with reflected light gave the most accurate measurement of the time. Today, the accepted speed of light is 186,282 miles per second through the vacuum of space.

As it turns out, light is the fastest thing we know about. If you could ride your bicycle at the speed of light, you would travel around the earth seven times in one second! That's about 880,000 times faster than sound's average speed in air of 1,100 feet per second. (That's why you see lightning so much sooner than you hear its thunder.)

Light, can be slowed down a little, however. It moves through a vacuum at its maximum speed. When it passes through a transparent material like air or water, its speed is different. Light moves faster through air than it moves through water and faster through water than it moves through glass. You can see this change of speed when light travels from one transparent material to another at an angle. The light bends or *refracts* at the boundary between the two materials. In this chapter you'll bend some light yourself and see some of the amazing effects of refraction.

MAKE MONEY APPEAR BEFORE YOUR EYES

Materials & Equipment

- an opaque cup or bowl

- a piece of transparent cellophane tape
- a coin
- a glass of water

Procedure

Tape the coin securely to the bottom of the inside of the cup or bowl. Move your head slowly away (back) from the cup until the coin is just beyond your view. Hold your head in this position as you carefully pour the water into the cup. The coin will reappear before your eyes.

Here's What's Happening

You can't see the coin because some of the light rays that come from the coin are blocked by the cup and the rest of the rays from the coin go above your eyes. When you put water in the cup, the light previously hitting your forehead bends down toward your eyes, and the coin comes into view.

THINKING OF LIGHT AS WAVES

Scientists could not explain some of the behavior of light by thinking about it as being made up of streams of particles. So they invented another way of thinking about light, describing it as being made up of waves. It's worth a little effort to think about what a wave is. In fact, we will give

light rays

light path after bend at surface of water

you a way to make waves and to study them in Chapter 9. But for now, use your imagination. If you drop a pebble into a still pond, the pebble causes waves that travel in ever-widening circles from the disturbance. The high point of each wave is the *crest*; the low point between crests is the *trough*. The distance from one crest to the next or from one trough to the next is called the *wavelength*. A wave is started by a pulse of energy, and it travels through time and space. Water waves are only a model for light waves. Light waves are similar to water waves because they are also made up of crests and troughs, but light wavelengths are ten million times smaller than water wavelengths. And light doesn't need a medium, like water, to travel through. Light travels through the vacuum of space.

Refraction can be explained if we think of light as being made up of waves. In the preceding experiment, when a wave of light from the coin reaches the water-air boundary at an angle, one part of the wave enters the air before the other parts. This part of the wave speeds up because light travels faster in air than in water. The other parts of the light wave that are still in the water are traveling at a slower speed than the part in the air. This happens to each part of the wave as it leaves the water, and this change in speed causes the light to bend.

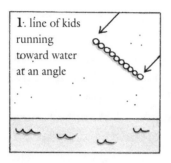

1. line of kids running toward water at an angle

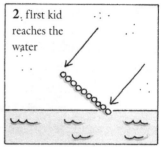

2. first kid reaches the water

3. kids in the water are slowing down

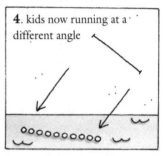

4. kids now running at a different angle

Here's another way you can think about this. Imagine that you are with ten of your friends at the beach, and you all stand in a row to race toward the water. If you all ran toward the sea at the same speed and reached the water all at the same time, the water would slow all of you down at the same moment. But suppose that your lineup heads for the water at an angle. Jim, your friend on one end of the line, reaches the water before Kristin, who is standing next to him. And Kristin reaches it before the friend next to her, and so on. As each person hits the water, he or she slows down. By the time everyone is in the water, the whole line is running more slowly in another direction.

This is what happens to light waves: If light meets a boundary between two materials head-on, it will pass from one to the other without changing direction. When it strikes the boundary between transparent materials at an angle, it refracts.

False Pencils in Water

Materials & Equipment
- a clear glass
- water
- a pencil
- a square or rectangular clear-glass baking dish

Procedure

Put water in the glass. Stick the pencil in the water and look at it from the side. Notice that the part of the pencil in the water is displaced from the part of the pencil that is in the air. Hold

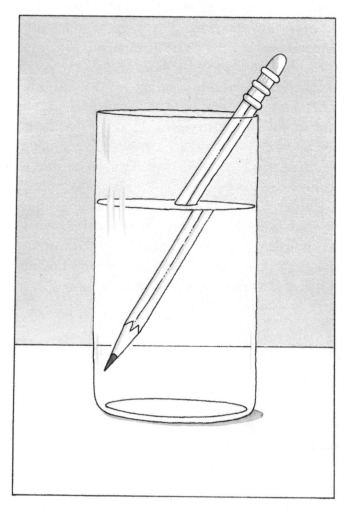

the pencil at a slant and look down on it from the top. Notice that the image of the pencil under water appears to be shorter than the pencil actually is.

Put water in the baking dish until it is almost full. Rest the eraser end of the pencil on one edge of the dish about one inch from the corner. Hold the point of the pencil under the water so that it touches the bottom of the dish. Look at the pencil from about one foot away and slowly lower your head. You should see two images of the pencil. If your eye level drops below the sur-

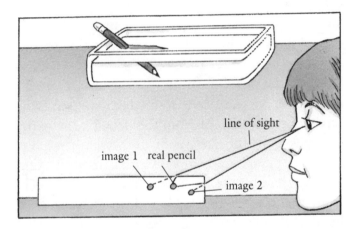

face of the water, you have gone too far, and you should slowly raise your head.

Here's What's Happening

The image of the pencil looks displaced when it is in water because the light coming from the pencil is bent as it leaves the glass and enters the air. The light coming from the pencil underwater is taking a different path than it would take if the pencil were completely in air. The light from the part of the pencil that is underwater travels to your eye at an angle, as the light is bent. Your eyes don't perceive the bend, however. You see the pencil as if the light were coming from a straight-line extension of the line of sight from your eyes back into the water. The pencil appears shorter for the same reason. The light bends, and the apparent length of the pencil is shorter than the actual length. For the same reason, when you look down at a person standing in the shallow end of a swimming pool, the legs appear to be abnormally short for the person's body.

When the pencil is in the baking dish, there is a range of eye positions from which you see two separate paths of light from the pencil. One path emerges from the surface of the water. The rays from the pencil are bent down toward your eyes at the water-air boundary. The other path emerges from the side of the baking dish. Its rays also bend as they emerge from the glass, but at a different angle. Since the light that comes from the top of the water has a different angle from that of the light coming from the side of the dish, you see a pencil in two different locations under the water—you see two separate underwater images.

HOT-AIR MIRAGES . . . WITHOUT A DESERT!

Procedure

This is something to watch for on a sunny, hot summer day. When you happen to be on a long, straight road, take a look at the surface of the road up ahead of the car. It often appears that there are pools of water on the road. You may even see the "reflections" of cars in these "pools."

When you drive closer to these "pools," you will see that they disappear. You have been the

victim of a mirage. This is the same illusion that fools many thirsty wanderers in the desert.

Here's What's Happening

Glass and water are not the only substances that can bend light. The temperature of the air affects the speed of light also. When light travels through air of one temperature into air of another, its speed changes, and the light bends.

The air near the ground is much hotter than the air higher up. Light that is coming from above is refracted when it meets this hotter air. Instead of continuing in its path toward the road, the light is bent up toward your eyes. You see an image of the blue sky where you would normally see the road. It looks as if the road is covered with a pool of water. Often you can see what appears to be the reflection of the car as if the car is driving on water. This is not a reflection at all, but a bending of the light as it meets different air temperatures.

LOSE A GLASS IN A GLASS

Materials & Equipment
- a clear glass jar free of labels or other marking patterns
- a smaller clear glass jar that fits inside the larger one
- paint thinner—also known as petroleum distil-

cooler air

warmer air

image of the sky reflected
back to driver's eyes

late (Caution: We suggest you use this substance only with an adult present—it is poisonous and can also burn your skin or eyes. Use
in a well-ventilated place, because the fumes

can be harmful. Be sure there are no open flames in the room, as this substance is flammable.)

Procedure

Put the smaller jar into the larger one. Fill the smaller jar and the space between the two jars with paint thinner. The small jar seems to simply disappear.

When you are finished with the experiment, carefully pour the paint thinner back into its original container and seal tightly.

Here's What's Happening

The speed of light through any transparent material is always slower than the speed of light in a vacuum. Scientists have measured the speed of light in many transparent materials. They have assigned specific numbers to a variety of materials. The numbers compare the speed of light in each of the different materials with the speed of light in a vacuum. This number is called the material's *index of refraction*. The index of refraction is also a measure of how much a material will bend light. A material that has a high index of refraction, like a diamond, will bend light more than a material with a lower index of refraction, like water.

You can see a boundary line between two transparent materials only when they have different indexes of refraction. It's easy to see the edges of a glass jar in air. You see the outlines of the smaller jar when it is inside the larger one because it is surrounded by air. Paint thinner has an index of refraction that is very close to the index of refraction of glass. When you replace the air with paint thinner, the light is no longer bent at the boundary of the inner glass, and you can no longer see its outline.

Chapter Four

LIGHT BENDERS

A lens is a curved piece of transparent material. It refracts the light rays coming from an object so that they meet, or *focus*, to form an image of the object. The lens in your eye focuses light from an object so that it forms an image on the *retina* at the back of the eye, where light-sensitive nerves send a message to your brain. Most ordinary vision problems are caused by a failure to focus a clear image on the retina. A nearsighted person has trouble seeing objects that are far away. The images of distant objects are focused in front of the retina. A farsighted person has trouble seeing close-up objects, such as printed words in a book. The images of nearby objects are focused behind the retina. In both cases, the retina is not located where the focused images fall. Eyeglasses are refracting optical instruments that correct for these conditions.

The first human-made lenses were probably fragments of clear blown glass that were smooth enough and round enough to improve someone's vision. The first person to look through them probably was a glassblower living in Pisa, Italy, around 1280. Imagine how excited you would be if you couldn't read a word on a page until you looked through a piece of glass and suddenly you could read again! Inexpensive glass lenses that were ground and polished soon followed. People involved in printing and religious scholars were among the first to benefit from magnifiers that improved their eyesight.

The first spectacles (from the Latin word *spectare* meaning "to watch"), or "disks for the eyes," were heavy glass disks with a double convex (outwardly curving) shape that magnified close work and corrected farsighted vision. In the middle of the fourteenth century, Italians called them "glass lentils" because their shape was like that of the lentil bean. The word "lens" evolved from *lenticchia*, Italian for "lentil." Good ideas also travel. By the beginning of the fifteenth century, spectacles were being used in China. By this time, back in Italy, lenses with a double concave (inwardly curving) surface, to correct for nearsightedness, became available, but only to the wealthy, since improvement to make distant vision clearer was considered a luxury. The extravagant sixteenth-century pope

Nearsightedness

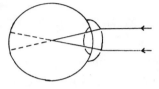

The eyeball is too long for light rays from a distant object to focus on the retina.

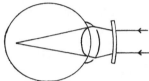

Glasses with concave lenses correct nearsightedness. The lenses force the light rays to travel farther through the eyeball to be focused on the retina.

Farsightedness

The eyeball is too short for light rays from nearby objects to be focused on the retina.

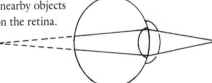

Glasses with convex lenses start to refract the light rays before they reach the eye. The light rays then focus on the retina.

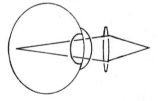

Leo X wore spectacles to improve his marksmanship when hunting.

As people grow older, their eyes fail to adjust from distance focusing to focusing on reading. In the eighteenth century, Benjamin Franklin (1706–1790) invented bifocal lenses so that when he was traveling, he could look up from his reading and see the scenery. Bifocals became common in the 1820's, about forty years after Franklin invented them.

The first person to conceive of corrective contact lenses was the great Italian painter and inventor Leonardo da Vinci (1452–1519). He designed a short, water-filled tube with a glass lens sealing one end. The water in the tube would be the part that actually rested on the eyeball. Da Vinci's lenses were not practical, however, and remained only an idea that was ahead of its time, like so many of his projects. Wearable glass contact lenses were invented in 1877 by Dr. A. E. Fick, a Swiss doctor. They were hard, thick and very uncomfortable. But they proved that people could get used to discomfort in the interest of correcting their vision. Today's extremely comfortable extended-wear soft contact lenses are 80 percent water, which duplicates, as closely as possible, the actual surface of the eye.

As lens grinders refined their art, one of these craftsmen, twenty-one-year-old Dutch optician

Hans Lippershey (1587–1619), made an amazing discovery. When he looked through two particular lenses that were lined up and adjusted to the right positions, distant objects seemed closer. Lippershey mounted the lenses in a tube, and in 1608 the telescope came into being. The Dutch government instantly saw potential for the telescope in warfare and tried to keep it a secret. But word got out to Galileo, who figured out how to make his own telescope within months of hearing about it. Galileo used his telescope to look at the heavens, and the science of astronomy took off.

The microscope, also composed of two lenses, was invented at just about the same time by another Dutchman, Zacharias Janssen (1588–1632). Other people refined it, and by the middle of the seventeenth century, the microscope was revealing the wonders of the world too tiny for human vision to perceive. An Italian doctor, Marcello Malpighi (1628–1694), studied the lungs of frogs, the wings of bats, chick embryos, and insects under the microscope. He showed that the microscopic realm was at least as complex and fascinating as the world of astronomy, and he is considered the father of modern microscopy. The telescope and the microscope extended the limits of human perception and made possible two new sciences.

In this chapter you will use lenses to perform some amazing experiments.

A Light Bender in Action

Materials & Equipment
- a shoe box without the top
- scissors
- a comb
- tape
- a magnifying glass
- sunlight coming through a window

Procedure

Cut a rectangular hole in the center of one end of the shoe box. It should be slightly wider than the diameter of the magnifying glass. Its height should be slightly less than the length of the comb's teeth. Make a slot, as thick as the magnifying glass and as wide as its diameter, in the bottom of the shoe box, parallel to the end, and about three inches from the hole. The purpose of the slot is to hold the magnifying glass so it is facing the end of the shoe box. Tape the comb over the opening at the end of the box. Put the lens in the slot so that half of it is sticking above the bottom of the box. Move the shoe box near the window so the sunlight streams into it through the comb. Tilt the box back and forth and watch the rays of light on the bottom of the

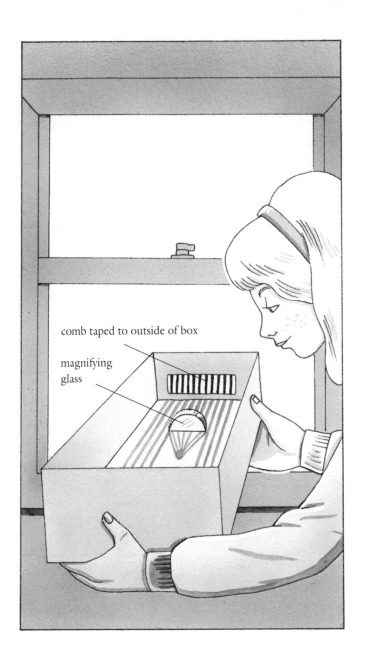

comb taped to outside of box

magnifying glass

box as they bend past the lens.

Here's What's Happening

A magnifying glass is a lens with two *convex* (bulging) surfaces. Light bends to different degrees depending upon what part of the lens the light strikes. In the center of the lens, the glass is flat. At the edges, the glass is curved. A ray of light that hits the center of the lens is not bent and passes straight through. Rays that strike the outer parts of the lens are bent more because they hit the glass surface at a steeper angle. The

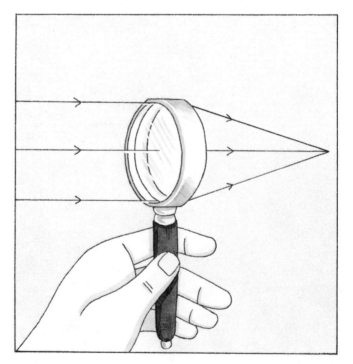

rays are bent again as they emerge from the other side of the lens.

In this experiment, the teeth of the comb separate the light into parallel rays that are easy to see. The light rays enter the shoe box, pass through the lens, and are bent. Instead of moving in parallel lines, the rays are now converging. They will meet at a common point some distance from the lens. This point is called the *focal point.*

WATCH TV UPSIDE DOWN ON A PIECE OF PAPER

Material & Equipment
- a magnifying glass
- a piece of white paper
- a television

Procedure
You can make an image with your magnifying glass of almost anything: a window with the sun shining through it, a tree outside in your yard, or even the dog in your neighbor's yard. However, these are rather boring things to look at, especially when your home contains something much more entertaining. One of the greatest image-generating sources in your house is the television set.

Turn off the lights, tune your TV to your favorite show, and stand back about ten feet from the set. Hold the lens in one hand and the paper in the other. Position the lens vertically between the TV and the paper and hold the paper about six inches from the lens. Both the lens and the paper should be parallel to the TV screen and at right angles to the floor. Move the paper away from and toward the lens until you see a focused image of your television picture. Sit back and watch the show—but you may have to turn your head upside down, because the image is inverted and backward.

If you are not satisfied with the size of your image, you can change the magnification by changing your distance from the TV set. Try

Light rays spread out from TV.

standing twenty feet from the set and then try
two feet.

Here's What's Happening

When light leaves a point on the TV, it spreads
out in many different directions. As a result,
light from one point on the TV hits the entire
surface of the magnifying lens. The lens then
bends and redirects this light so that it comes
back together again as a single point. This happens to every point of light that makes up the
image on the TV screen. In this way, the TV image is reconstructed by the lens.

The lens bends light from the left portion of

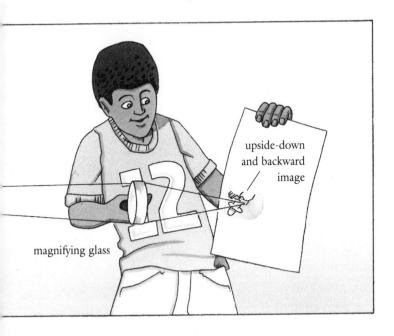

upside-down
and backward
image

magnifying glass

the TV, redirecting it to the right portion of the image, and the right portion to the left. Light from the top of the TV gets redirected to the bottom of the image and vice versa. As a result, the image is upside down and backward.

You may notice that when you are closer to the TV, you have to hold the paper farther from the lens to find a clear image than when you are farther away from the TV. The location of the focal point of a lens determines the size of the image and the distance of the image from the lens for any particular distance to the object.

A REAR-PROJECTION PROJECTOR

Materials & Equipment
- a magnifying glass
- a shoe box with a lid
- scissors
- tape
- tracing paper

Procedure
Cut an eight-inch slot down the center of the bottom of the shoe box just wide enough for the handle of the magnifying glass. In the center of one end of the shoe box cut an opening (it can be square or round) that is slightly larger than the diameter of the magnifying glass. Cut off the

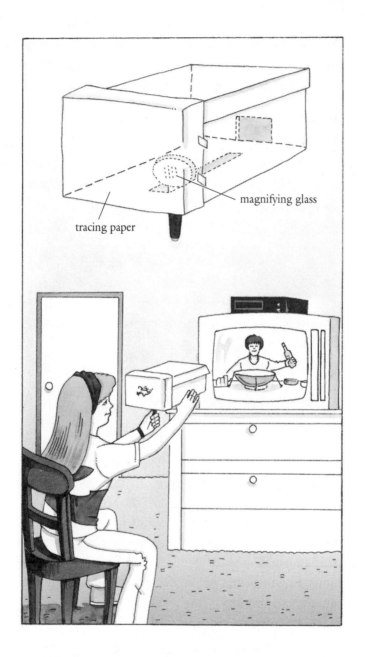

magnifying glass

tracing paper

other end of the shoe box. Tape a piece of tracing paper to this end of the shoe box to form a screen. Place the magnifying glass in the slot and hold the handle so that the glass's surface is parallel to the ends of the box. Put the cover on the shoe box.

To use your projector, point the open hole toward some object, such as your TV screen. Watch the tracing paper. Move the lens back and forth in the slot until you get a clear image on the screen. This image will be upside down like the one in the previous experiment. However, since the image is projected from the rear, it is correctly oriented from left to right. You'll still have to watch TV upside down on your rear-projection screen, but you won't have to read the words backward.

THE SWIMMING-POOL EFFECT

Procedure

The focusing effect of a lens is something that occurs in nature quite often. In fact, every time you go swimming in a pool or lake, beams of sunlight are being focused all around you. This is one of those common sights most people never stop to think about. However, after this experiment a swimming pool will never look quite the same to you again.

Look down at the floor of a pool. You should

see bright lines of light making wild patterns all over the floor. If you do not see them, throw in a small stone. Now you should see rings of light on the bottom of the pool just beneath the area where the stone was thrown.

Since water and air are different substances, the light changes its speed when it enters the water, and it bends. However, the ripples on the surface of the water are curved just as the surface of a lens is curved. The ripples actually focus sunlight into bright lines or patterns on the floor of the pool.

Every time a ripple or wave is made, light is focused somewhere in the pool. You can see the patterns change as the ripples move. We'll put the swimming-pool effect to work in Chapter 9, when we study wave motion using a ripple tank.

An Ice Lens

Every optical instrument, from binoculars to cameras to eyeglasses, contains lenses that were made by opticians. You can discover basic lens-making techniques in the next two experiments.

Materials & Equipment
- a tennis ball
- a sharp knife
- vegetable oil
- a small juice glass

- distilled water (from the supermarket or drugstore)
- a freezer
- a magazine

Procedure

Ask an adult to help you cut the tennis ball in half with the knife. Dip your finger in the oil and put a thin coating of oil on the inside of one of the halves of the tennis ball. The oil coating will make it easier to remove your ice lens from its mold without breaking it. Set the tennis-ball mold in the glass, hollow side up, and adjust it until it is level. Then fill the oiled mold with distilled water until the surface of the water is even with the rim of the ball. The lens should be as close to being a perfect hemisphere as possible. Put the glass, ball, and water in the freezer. Check every few hours to see if the water is frozen and clear. If you leave it in the freezer for too long, it may get cloudy.

When the lens is frozen, pop it out of the tennis ball. Rub your hand over the flat part of the lens to smooth out any rough areas. Hold the lens over a magazine with the curved side facing your eyes to make things look bigger. Hold the curved side of the lens toward your TV, and try to project an image of the TV on a piece of paper.

Here's What's Happening

Opticians make lenses by pouring hot molten glass or plastic into molds. The water magnifying lens does not make as clear an image as a lens made out of glass. (You may have noticed this when you tried to use it to watch TV on a piece of paper.) However, the fuzzy image has more to do with the shape of the lens than with the material from which it's made—the ice lens has a much rounder curve than a glass magnifying lens. In most cases, when a magnifying lens has too rounded a curve, the image will be poor.

Very skilled craftspeople also make lenses by grinding glass into curved shapes. See this process for yourself in the next experiment.

GRINDING AN ICE LENS

Materials & Equipment

- ice cubes
- the other tennis ball half from the previous experiment
- hot running water

Procedure

Find an ice cube that is as clear as possible (you might want to make it from distilled water). Run hot water on the inside of the tennis ball half so that it gets warm. Put the ice cube in the ball and move it around on the inside of the ball's curve. About every ten seconds take the ice cube out and warm up the ball again. Put the ice cube back into the ball and repeat these steps until your ice cube has a curved surface. Use your ice lens as a magnifier, or use it to do some of the other lens experiments in this chapter.

Here's What's Happening

When you rub the cube in the warm curve of the ball, the outside of the ice cube melts to fit the shape of the curve. An optician grinds a lens using a similar procedure, except that the glass isn't melted; it is ground down by abrasive materials. An optician starts out with a very rough abrasive on a curved piece of metal and rubs the glass until it takes on the curve of the metal. As grinding continues and the lens takes shape, the abrasive is changed to a finer and finer grade. When the polishing stage is reached, the abrasive is almost smooth. Opticians have been grinding lenses this way for hundreds of years. Although there are a few machines that take the place of some of the hand grinding, the entire process is still very time-consuming, and it requires patience.

Chapter Five

BOUNCING LIGHT

Why can't you see in the dark? If that seems like a dumb question, try this: Why can't you see when a light shines directly into your eyes? All you see is a lot of light, and it hurts. You don't see any objects. Here's another: Why does a telephone look different from a toothbrush? These are the kinds of "dumb" questions a scientist asks. When scientists try to answer questions like these, they invent ideas that can be tested and proved by doing experiments. The idea that answers all these questions is: We see things because light bounces off the surfaces of objects into our eyes. We can't see in the dark because there is no light to bounce. When light shines directly into our eyes, it doesn't bounce off anything, so we don't see anything. A telephone appears to be different from a toothbrush because light bounces off each object differently.

This chapter is about a fundamental property

of light: its ability to bounce. The bouncing of light is called *reflection*. A mirror is an example of a material that reflects nearly all the light that strikes it. The light that bounces off a mirror bounces in a special way that makes it different from the light that bounces off other objects. Do the next experiment to discover what this is.

TURN ON YOUR TV FROM ANOTHER ROOM

The remote-control device for your television or VCR uses an invisible light called *infrared radiation*. (We'll tell you more about invisible light in Chapter 8.) Invisible light behaves the same way visible light behaves. Infrared light travels in straight lines and can be refracted and reflected. We can't see it because our eyes are not equipped to detect it. However, a remote-control television has an infrared-light detector on it. When you produce the infrared signal with the remote-control device, the detector picks up the signal and triggers the television to do something. This experiment uses the remote-control infrared beam to illustrate how a mirror reflects light.

Materials & Equipment
- a television or VCR with a wireless remote control (make sure the batteries in the remote control are still very fresh)

- several hand mirrors
- a willing friend—more if possible

Procedure

Turn your back to the appliance and use a hand mirror to look at it. Hold the remote control up level with your eyes and aim into the mirror at the small square or round light detector on the front of the set. Press the on/off button. When the television or VCR goes on, use the same technique to change the channel and volume.

Now try something a little more spectacular: Stand out in the hall or in the room next to the TV room. Have a friend hold a mirror at the entrance of the room so that you can see the TV or VCR in the mirror. Aim for the image of the detector in the mirror and turn on the set.

Now try this: Turn your back to your friend's mirror and use another mirror to see the first mirror. Line up the infrared detector in both mirrors, aim the remote control, and fire! You can use as many mirrors and friends as you want as long as you can line up images to see the detector. See if you can find a limit to the number of mirrors and people you use before you can no longer turn on the TV.

Here's What's Happening

The surface of a mirror reflects light in much

the same way that a ball bounces off a gym floor. If you throw a ball straight down, it bounces straight up. If you throw it at an angle, it bounces away from you at an angle equal to the one it struck the floor at. Light behaves the same way. Light bounces away from a mirror at the same angle as it strikes the mirror. Also, the rays of light coming off an object are not scattered as they bounce off a flat mirror. This kind of orderly reflection is called *specular reflection*. You use specular reflection to see your own image behind the surface of a mirror. It can also be used to see around corners.

OFF-THE-WALL TV CONTROL

If the batteries in your remote control are fresh you don't have to have perfect aim to turn on your TV. Try this experiment to see what your walls do to light.

Materials & Equipment
- a television or VCR with a wireless remote control (with very fresh batteries in the remote control)
- walls and a ceiling

Procedure
Point your remote control toward the ceiling

of your TV room and try to turn on the appliance. Try pointing it at different walls to turn it on. Turn your back to the TV, aim for the back wall, and see what happens. Find out when it works and when it doesn't.

Here's What's Happening

Walls reflect lots of light, but they don't reflect it in the same way a mirror does. Walls are not specular reflectors; they are *diffuse* reflectors. Nearly everything you see is a diffuse reflector. Here's the difference. Imagine that you have ten small rubber balls in your hand. If you throw them down on a smooth surface (such as a basketball court), they will all bounce away from you at about the same angle at which they hit the floor. If you throw the same balls on a rough surface (such as your bedroom floor before your mother makes you clean up your room), all the balls will bounce, but one ball might hit a video-game cartridge, one might hit your belt buckle, one might hit the sole of your shoe, and one might bounce off this book. The balls will be sent flying off in all different directions. Light bounces off a specular surface much the same way balls bounce off the basketball court, and it bounces off diffuse surfaces the way the balls bounce off your messy bedroom floor.

The infrared detector on your TV or VCR is

triggered only if it receives enough infrared light. Almost all the light that bounces off a specular reflector can be redirected toward the detector. But a diffuse reflector sends the light out in all different directions. If the remote control is positioned just right, enough reflected light reaches the detector and the TV responds. But if the diffusely reflected light is not "bright" enough, the detector is not activated.

WATCH TV WITH A CURVED MIRROR

You can use a curved mirror to project an image on a small piece of paper or index card. A shaving mirror or makeup mirror is curved so that your face appears magnified when you look into it. Most drugstores carry inexpensive magnifying mirrors.

Materials & Equipment
- a shaving or makeup mirror
- a television
- a 2-inch-square piece of paper or a small index card

Procedure
Turn out the lights, turn on your television, and stand about twenty feet from the screen.

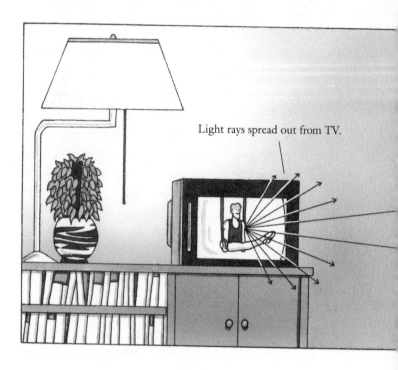

Light rays spread out from TV.

Face the curved side of the mirror toward the television and hold the card between the television and the mirror about one foot from the mirror. Slowly move the card back and forth until you see the image of the television reflected from the mirror onto the card.

The image should look very similar to the image that you made with the magnifying lens in the last chapter. However, there is something else that you can do with the curved mirror that can't be done with the magnifying lens. Try the next experiment.

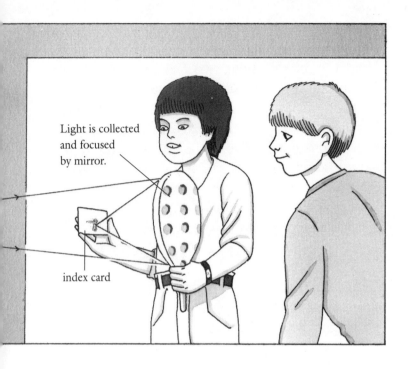

Light is collected and focused by mirror.

index card

Make a Big-Screen TV with a Curved Mirror

You may have noticed in Chapter 4, when you watched TV upside down on a piece of paper, that the image that was formed with the magnifying lens changed its size depending on how far from the television you were standing. The closer you stand, the larger the image. The same properties apply to the curved mirror.

Position the television so that there is a blank, light-colored wall directly behind it. (*Be sure to*

ask permission before you move the television.)
Hold the mirror about two feet in front of the
TV and tilt it slightly upward to project an image
on the wall. Move the mirror toward and away
from the TV to get the image in focus. If you
want to change the size of the image on the wall,
move the television closer or farther away from
the wall.

SEE THE ASTIGMATISM IN A CURVED MIRROR

Materials & Equipment
• a shaving or makeup mirror
• a bright light

Procedure
For the best results, this experiment should be
done using the sun as a light source. Have an
adult go with you to an empty driveway or parking lot where there is no chance of anything
catching fire. (Focused sunlight can get very
hot.) On a sunny day, hold the magnifying side of
the curved mirror away from you at an angle so
that the bright reflected focus of the sunlight hits
the ground. *(Caution: Be very careful not to look
directly at the reflection of the sun in the mirror,
as this can damage your eyes.)* Experiment with
the position of the mirror. When you move it up
and down, you should see the focused image of

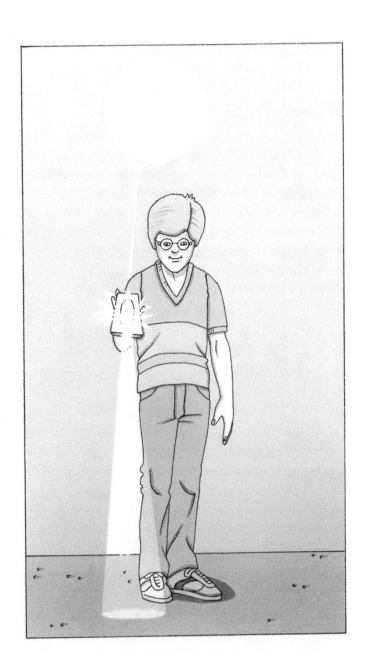

the sun on the ground turn from a bright vertical line to a bright horizontal line. The fact that the image is not a round point all the time is caused by a defect in the image called *astigmatism*. At one point, in the transition from vertical to horizontal images, the image is a circle. Scientists call this the "circle of least confusion," which says something about understanding astigmatism.

If it is not a sunny day, you can show the same property of the curved mirror by putting a bright lamp in one room. Turn off all other lights and go as far away from the lamp as you can (preferably to another room). Use the mirror to focus the lamplight onto the floor and move the mirror up and down. You should see the focus go from a bright horizontal line to a bright vertical line as described above.

Here's What's Happening

Ordinary lenses and mirrors such as your magnifying glass and curved mirror do not form perfect images. For a lens or mirror to make a perfect image, all the rays of light coming from a point on an object would have to be focused together at a point on the image. In fact, no lens or mirror is capable of making a truly perfect image, although some get very close. Image defects are called *aberrations*. They arise from all curved surfaces in both lenses and mirrors. There are many forms of aberrations, one of which is astigmatism.

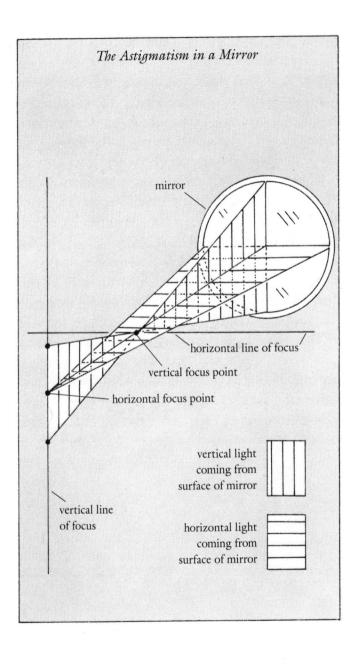

The Astigmatism in a Mirror

mirror

horizontal line of focus

vertical focus point

horizontal focus point

vertical line
of focus

vertical light
coming from
surface of mirror

horizontal light
coming from
surface of mirror

Astigmatism often becomes apparent when light hits a curved mirror or lens at a very sharp angle. Rays that strike the mirror in vertical lines focus in one spot, and rays that strike in horizontal lines focus in a different spot. As you move the mirror up and down through the focus, you see a horizontal line of light where the vertical rays have focused and a vertical line of light where the horizontal rays have focused. In order to understand this, you really have to do the experiment.

Some people have a defect in their eyes that is also called an astigmatism. Astigmatism in the eyes is caused by an abnormality in the shape of the cornea, which is the clear protective coating of the eyeball. An astigmatic eye has a cornea with a vertical curve that is different than the horizontal curve. This causes the vertical and horizontal focuses of the rays of light to be different. One effect of an astigmatism is that stars at night appear as lines of light rather than points.

Chapter Six

·

GUIDING LIGHT

A diamond sparkles because light bounces off the inside of its back surfaces. A diamond is cut so that it has many surfaces at different angles to each other. When the diamond is moved, the back surfaces reflect light to your eyes, and you see them as flashes. This is an example of *total internal reflection*, or *TIR*. Diamonds are not the only matter that exhibits TIR. Glass and water also reflect light internally. In this chapter you'll explore total internal reflection, which is the principle behind fiber optics—a technology in which light travels through glass fibers. Glass optical fibers can make light travel around corners, in circles, through cables across the country, down an esophagus to light up a stomach—to any place we might wish to guide it. Fiber-optic cables can carry far more information than electrical wires and are causing a transformation in world communication. In medicine, fiber optics are used to literally shed light on hard-to-see parts of the body. In the next experiment you make light travel around the corner of a baking dish.

SEND LIGHT THROUGH A GLASS BAKING DISH

Materials & Equipment
• a rectangular clear glass baking dish
• a flashlight
• a clear glass measuring cup
• a bowl of water

Procedure

Place the glass baking dish on a level surface and shine the flashlight down on one rim of the dish. Look through the rim of the dish on the side opposite from the flashlight. Move the flashlight back and forth along the rim and follow the light that appears on the rim of the other side.

Hold the measuring cup in one hand while you send the light from the flashlight down through the rim of the cup. Put your eyes close to the rim of the cup and look for the light coming up through the glass. You will find the emerging light coming up the side opposite the flashlight. After you find the light, put the bottom of the

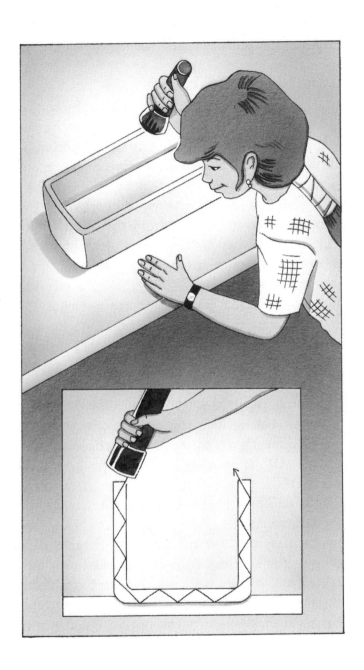

cup into the bowl of water. See the light dim.

Here's What's Happening

In Chapter 3 we discussed how light bends. When light crosses a boundary between two transparent substances such as glass and air, it bends away from a line (the *normal line*) perpendicular to the boundary. As the angle of light hitting the boundary becomes sharper, the light bends farther and farther from the normal line. Finally it reaches an angle (the *critical angle*) where it no longer exits into the other transparent medium. Instead, at the critical angle, the light is reflected back inside the material it's traveling through. In other words, the light is completely reflected inside the substance and not refracted. The reflection is the total internal reflection (TIR) we mentioned earlier.

Some of the light you shine through the rim of the glass baking dish reaches this critical angle. As the light travels down through the edge into the glass of the dish, some of it hits the boundary between the glass and the air at the critical angle and is reflected back into the glass. Because of the large difference in the index of refraction between glass and air (which means a large difference in the speed of light in each medium) this critical angle is not difficult to achieve. The light is reflected off the glass-air surface back into the baking dish, where it travels until it hits the next

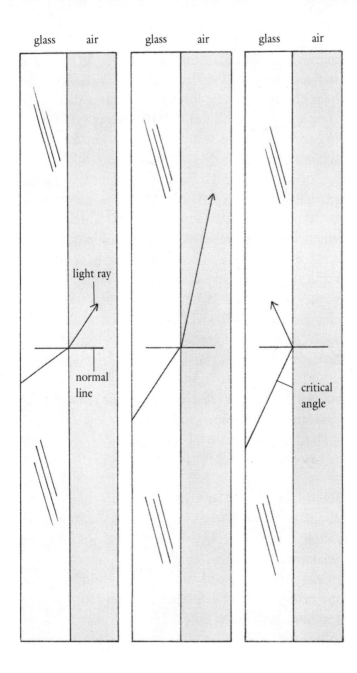

glass-air surface. It hits that surface at the same critical angle and reflects internally again. This happens all the way through the glass dish until it exits out the other end, where your eye is waiting to see it. Amazingly, TIR light bends around the corners of the dish.

Total internal reflection also happens with the glass measuring cup. Again, TIR is determined by the difference between glass and air. But when you put the bottom of the cup in water, the situation changes. The difference between the refractive index of water and that of the glass is not as great as the difference between the refractive indexes of air and glass. The critical angle is more difficult to reach. When the light reaches the glass-water surface, the angle is not sharp enough for all the light to bounce off the internal surface. Some of the light passes through the glass into the water, and the remaining TIR light is dramatically reduced.

Here's how TIR works in fiber optics: Optical fibers are very thin flexible rods of glass (around the thickness of a hair on your head) that are surrounded by another transparent material of much lower refractive index. Since light travels relatively slowly through the glass fiber and at a much greater speed through the surrounding material, there is perfect opportunity for total internal reflection to take place.

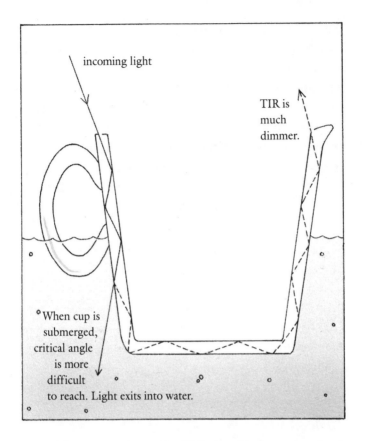

incoming light

TIR is
much
dimmer.

When cup is
submerged,
critical angle
is more
difficult
to reach. Light exits into water.

Light is sent into the fiber, and it bounces back and forth inside the fiber all the way to the other end, which is sometimes hundreds of miles away! Pulses of light in a fiber-optic material can carry the same kind of information that is transmitted as electrical pulses in a copper wire. This information can be telephone conversations or data from computers and fax machines. A conventional copper wire can carry a few million electrical pulses each second. But an optical fiber can carry as many as 20 billion light pulses per second! Telephone companies are switching to fiber-optic cables (made of bundles of fiber-optic fibers) because they can handle huge numbers of conversations at one time, many more than conventional copper wires can carry. And fiber optics in computers will vastly increase the amount of information they can handle.

MAKE A COIN DISAPPEAR IN A BOWL OF WATER

Materials & Equipment
- a small coin (a penny or a dime)
- a medium-sized opaque cereal bowl filled with water
- a small, clear glass

Procedure
Place the coin in the bottom of the bowl of water. Lower the glass upside down into the bowl over the coin. Be careful not to tilt the glass, or water will get in. As you lower the glass, watch the coin at a slight angle through the glass (don't look straight through the top of the glass). The coin disappears right before your eyes!

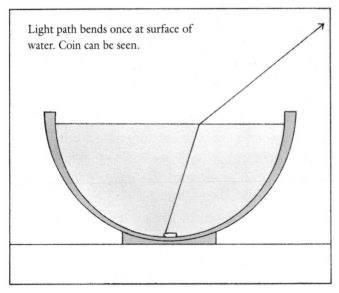

Light path bends once at surface of water. Coin can be seen.

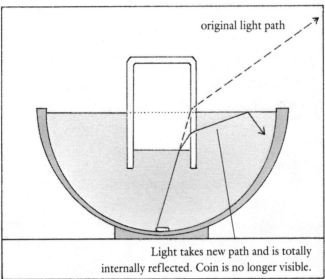

original light path

Light takes new path and is totally internally reflected. Coin is no longer visible.

Here's What's Happening

This is another trick of TIR. As you lower the glass, air in the glass pushes down the water level over the coin. The lower water level means that light from the coin leaves the water sooner and therefore bends sooner. The light then bends again through the glass and again into the water. The second time the light enters the water, it is at the critical angle to the surface of the water, and it is totally internally reflected at the water-air boundary. Since all the light from the coin is internally reflected, you can't see it. If you let the glass fill with water, TIR does not take place, and you continue to see the coin.

WIPE AWAY THE IMAGE OF A COIN WITH YOUR HAND

Materials & Equipment

- a small clear glass of water
- a coin

Procedure

Place a coin on the bottom of the glass filled with water. Hold the glass about a foot from your eyes and slightly below them so that your line of sight is at a slight angle above the surface of the water. You should see a magnified image of the coin appearing to float near the surface of the water. Place your dry hand on the opposite side of the glass and see if the image disappears. Now wet your hand and again place it on the back side of the glass.

Here's What's Happening

This is a combination of TIR and image formation with a curved mirror. Since light travels

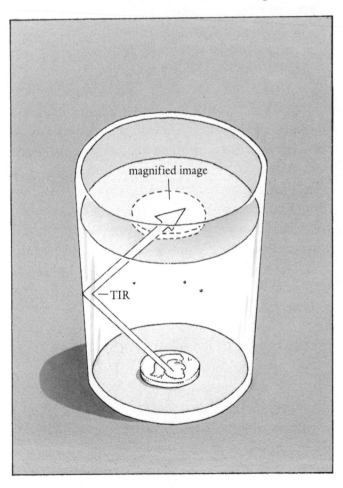

magnified image

TIR

more slowly in water and glass than it does in air, much of the light coming off the coin in the bottom of the glass has a very good chance of being internally reflected when it reaches the glass-air boundary. In addition, the surface of the glass is curved, so the internally reflected light behaves in a way that is similar to light reflected from a curved mirror.

The light coming from the coin hits the curved glass-air boundary at the critical angle. The reflection of the coin from the curved glass forms a magnified TIR image of the coin near the surface of the water. When you place your dry hand on the back of the glass, the image still remains in view because there are enough air gaps between your hand and the glass to continue to produce TIR. However, when you place your wet hand on the glass, the water fills up the air gaps between your hand and the glass, and you no longer have a glass-air boundary; you have a glass-hand boundary! The light is absorbed in your hand, and the TIR does not take place. The image near the water's surface disappears.

TRANSPARENT GELATIN THAT LIGHT CANNOT GET THROUGH

Materials & Equipment

- a flavored gelatin dessert (preferably a light

color such as orange or lemon), made with water
- square or rectangular clear glass baking dish
- a flashlight (preferably a focusable flashlight, which can be adjusted so that all the light is focused into one bright spot or spread evenly throughout the field of illumination)

Procedure

Make the gelatin according to the instructions on the package, and pour into the glass baking dish. The gelatin should be at least two inches deep. Chill until firm. Turn off the lights. Place the dish on a level surface and shine the flashlight (tightly focused if possible) through one side of the dish. Look from the adjacent side at the light through the gelatin. You should see the beam passing through the gelatin and out the

other side of the dish. You should also be able to see the flashlight's bulb. Move the flashlight so that the light enters one side of the dish and hits the adjacent side. Looking from the top, you should now see the beam of light bounce off the glass and reflect back into the gelatin. Look through the gelatin and see if you can still see the flashlight's bulb.

Here's What's Happening

Gelatin contains very large protein molecules—large enough to scatter light. The molecules scatter the light in all directions, and you can see the beam in the gelatin much as you can see headlight beams in a fog. You can also see the angle the beam makes when it reaches the glass-air boundary and the critical angle when it is totally internally reflected. When the light is not at the critical angle, it passes through both the gelatin and the glass dish. If the light from the bulb of the flashlight is reflected off the side of the dish before it reaches your eyes, you will not see the bulb.

POURING LIGHT

Materials & Equipment
- a tall, slim jar (such as an olive jar) and lid
- a hammer
- a large nail

- tape
- water
- a flashlight
- a sheet of newspaper

Procedure

Remove the lid from the jar. With the hammer and nail, make two holes in the lid: a large hole near the rim on one side and a smaller hole near the rim on the opposite side. Put tape over the holes on the outside of the lid. Fill the jar three quarters full with water and screw on the top. Turn on the flashlight and put the bottom of the jar on top of the lit end. Wrap the flashlight and jar together in newspaper to form a light-tight tube. Turn out the lights. Pull the tape off the holes. Tilt the jar and light so that water pours out of the larger hole. (The smaller hole lets in air so that you can pour a steady stream.) Put your finger in the stream. Can you see a spot of light on your finger no matter which part of the stream falls on it?

Here's What's Happening

The light follows the curve of the stream of water because of TIR inside the boundaries of the stream. This happens because there is a large difference between the index of refraction of water and the index of refraction of air.

Chapter Seven

·

BREAKING UP LIGHT

In 1666, the English physicist Isaac Newton (1642–1727) passed a beam of sunlight through a triangular wedge of glass. The beam spread out into bands of colors: red, orange, yellow, green, blue, indigo, and violet. Each color faded into the next, and they always appeared in the same order. (It's easy to remember the sequence if you think of the first letters of the colors forming this name: ROY G. BIV.) The piece of glass is called a *prism*, and the bands of colors are known as the *visible spectrum*. Newton then passed the spectrum through a second prism. The bands converged, and white light emerged again. Newton correctly concluded that white light is composed of the colored light of the visible spectrum.

If we think of light as waves, then a measure of color is the wavelength. Red light has the longest wavelength of the visible spectrum, and violet has the shortest. Scientists sometimes refer to short wavelengths as blue light and longer wavelengths as red light.

Make a prism out of water in the next experiment and take a crack at breaking up light yourself.

A WATER PRISM

Materials & Equipment

- a large bowl of water
- a window with sunlight streaming through it
- a small mirror
- a piece of white paper

Procedure

Place the bowl of water near the window so that the sunlight shines in on it. Hold the mirror in the water and tilt it toward the light. Move the piece of paper around to try to catch the reflection from the mirror. You should be able to see a rainbow of colors on the paper.

Here's What's Happening

When sunlight travels through air, all the colors that compose the white sunlight are moving at the same speed. When the sunlight enters a different medium, such as water, its speed changes, and the light is refracted. However, the different

colors of the white light begin to travel at slightly different speeds when they enter another medium, so they are not all refracted in equal amounts. Violet light is slowed the most, so it bends the most. Green light is slowed slightly less than blue but more than yellow. Red is slowed least, and it bends the least. As a result, the white light separates into a spectrum. As the light reflects off the mirror, the spreading of the spectrum bands widens. By placing the paper in the right spot, you can observe all the brilliant colors of the visible spectrum.

Colored bands are produced whenever refraction occurs. But most of the time they are too small to be seen with the naked eye. They can show up as colored fringes in the image formed by a lens. These fringes are called *chromatic aberrations*, and correcting for them is a challenge for lens designers.

COLORED LIGHTS THROUGH WATER

Materials & Equipment

- a sink with a drain stopper
- the permanent light above the sink *(Caution: Do not use a portable lamp for this experiment. It is dangerous to touch any electric appliance when your hands are wet, and it would be hazardous if the lamp were to fall in the water.)*

- a small mirror

Procedure

Stop up the drain and fill the sink with water. Turn on the light. Put the mirror in the bottom of the sink and look at the reflection of the light in the mirror. See the halo of colored light around the bulb. Tilt the mirror and move your head to view the bulb at different angles. Find an angle where most of the color around the bulb disappears.

Here's What's Happening

As the white light from the bulb enters the water, the light is refracted and separates into a spectrum. When light crosses the boundary between the water and air at a large angle, the colors will spread more than when the angle is small. When you hold the mirror so that the light is reflected straight back to the bulb, there isn't enough of an angle for the light to bend much. It enters the water head-on, and it is reflected directly back. The halo is so small you may not be able to see it.

All the light from the bulb is broken up when it passes into the water. It is as if every point of light from the bulb becomes a spectrum. In the center of the reflection all of the spectra overlap.

The light remixes and appears white. At the edges of the reflection there is no overlap. The spectrum appears as colored fringes around the light bulb. The effect is similar to the penumbra of a shadow.

MAKE A RAINBOW IN YOUR BACKYARD

Materials & Equipment
- a garden hose with a spray nozzle
- a sunny day

Procedure
Stand with your back to the sun and spray as fine a mist as possible with the hose. Look for the rainbow in the air. Sometimes it helps if you stand on a blacktopped driveway.

Here's What's Happening
Each tiny water drop acts as a light bender and a light bouncer. Light is bent when it enters the drop, is internally reflected off the back of the drop and is bent again when it leaves the drop and reenters the air. Since the drop is round, the curved surface spreads out the emerging spectrum. The spread is so wide that each drop of water will show you only one color. You see only a band of red at the top of a rainbow because all the other colors from those drops are bent at angles that miss your eyes. Drops in the middle of the rainbow send yellow and green light into

your eyes, they bend the red light at an angle that passes under your eyes, and the blue, indigo, and violet light is bent so it passes over your eyes. The drops at the bottom of the rainbow can bend only the violet light so it meets your eyes.

A natural rainbow is a rare event. It depends on a variety of conditions. Both sunlight and rain must be present. The rainbow will appear in the part of the sky opposite to the sun. Raindrops act as tiny prisms, breaking up the sunlight into all the colors of the spectrum just as the drops from the hose do. Whether or not you see a rainbow depends on your position and the angle of the sun. At dawn and dusk a rainbow will be projected into the ground before it can reach our eyes. At noon, the rainbow is projected too high to see from the ground. But in the morning or afternoon, when the sun is at the right height, a rainbow can be visible. The rainbow you see from your position, however, will not be the same rainbow that is seen by a person standing next to you.

MAKE A SUNSET IN A GLASS OF WATER

Materials & Equipment
- a tall clear glass with water in it
- 1/2 teaspoon milk
- a flashlight

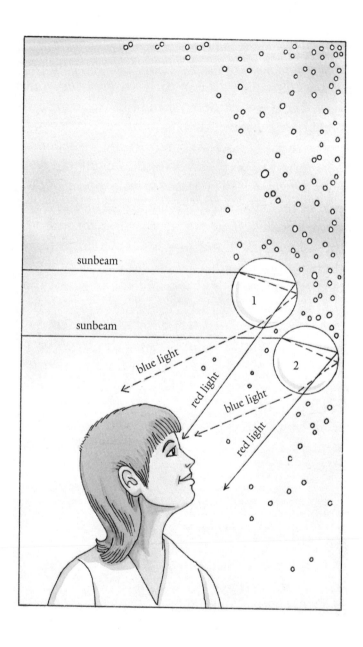

Procedure

Stir the milk into the water. Shine the flashlight through the side of the glass, and notice that the water-milk mixture takes on a bluish color. Look at the flashlight's bulb through the side of the glass. It should have a yellow-orange color. Now shine the flashlight from the bottom of the glass. Look down from the top of the glass, through the liquid, at the flashlight's bulb. It should be a much deeper orange color now.

Here's What's Happening

This experiment demonstrates why the sky is blue and a sunset is red and orange. Lord John W. S. Rayleigh, an English physicist (1842–1919), helped answer these questions. Rayleigh discovered that when light encounters a particle that is smaller than the light's wavelength, part of that light gets scattered by the particle. The particle is too small to reflect the light that strikes it, so through *diffraction* (which we will tell you more about in Chapter 9) the light bends around the particle in such a way that it is scattered in all different directions. A small particle (one that is smaller than the blue wavelength) will scatter more of the blue energy than it will red energy. Larger particles will either block or reflect the blue light. The end result is that blue light is more easily scattered than red light.

Milk particles in a glass of water are a model of

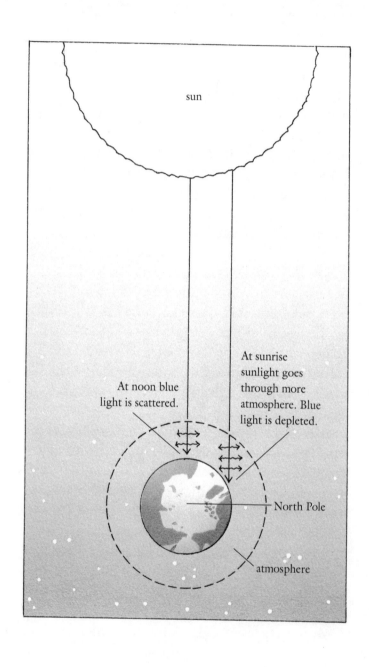

sun

At noon blue
light is scattered.

At sunrise
sunlight goes
through more
atmosphere. Blue
light is depleted.

North Pole

atmosphere

the atmosphere. The small particles of milk that are suspended in the water scatter the blue light that enters the liquid. When you look at the liquid from the side, it appears to be bluish. When you look at the light source through the liquid, it appears to be orange because there is less blue light left. Most of it has been scattered away. When more particles are added, or when the light goes through more liquid, not only is the blue light scattered but so is some green and a little orange. So when you look at the light source from the top of the glass, it appears to have a deeper orange color because it has passed through more liquid. Blue, green, and yellow wavelengths are scattered, leaving behind the darker red and orange wavelengths.

The earth's atmosphere is made up of gas molecules, dust particles, and water vapor. When sunlight travels through the atmosphere, the particles scatter the short wavelengths, which light up the sky, making it look blue. As the sun rises or sets on the horizon, the light must travel through more of the earth's atmosphere. As it does this, more of the blue light is depleted, and the sun appears to be orange.

Chapter Eight

COLOR

The human eye is capable of seeing the range of colors (from red to violet) that make up the visible spectrum. It also is capable of seeing thousands of shades in between. Take a look at the shades of lipstick or nail polish available at a local cosmetic store to get a sense of the variety of reds and pinks. The color of an opaque object depends on the kind of light that shines on it and on the light that is reflected by it. Since white light contains all the visible wavelengths, a white object reflects all the visible wavelengths. Black objects *absorb* nearly all the light that hits them, so very little light is reflected back to your eyes. Try this: On a hot sunny day, place a black shirt and a white shirt in the sun. Feel them fifteen minutes later and see which one is hotter. When light is absorbed, heat is produced. That's why white is worn in tropical climates. What happens to the colors of objects when colored light shines on them? Do the next experiment and find out.

MAKE A GREEN GUMBALL BLACK

Materials & Equipment

- a shoe box
- a ruler
- scissors
- cellophane of several different colors (from a gift store)
- tape
- several gumballs of different colors (white, red, blue, green, etc.)
- a strong light source or a sunny day

Procedure

Cut a rectangular hole in the top of the shoe box 3 inches wide by 6 inches long. Cut out a rectangular piece of red cellophane about 8 inches wide by 14 inches long. Fold it in half twice to produce a filter of four layers with a size of about 4 inches by 7 inches. Tape the red cellophane filter to the inside of the shoe-box top so that it completely covers the rectangular hole. Cut a 1-inch round hole in one end of the shoe box. Put the gumballs inside the shoe box and put on the cover. Go out in the sunshine or shine

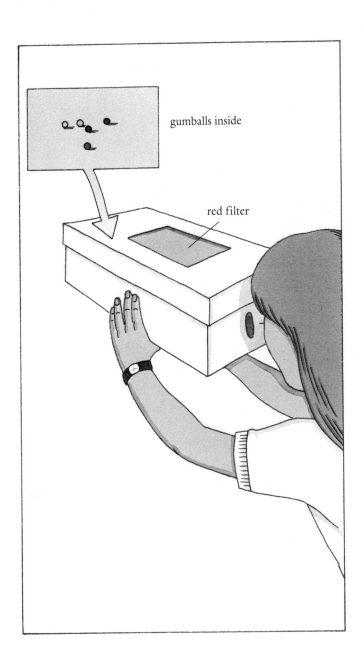

gumballs inside

red filter

a lamp through the cellophane. Look into the box through the round hole. See what colors the gumballs are. Repeat this experiment with different colors of cellophane.

Here's What's Happening

A red object appears red because it reflects mostly red light back to your eyes. All the other colors of visible light are absorbed into the object. When you put a red filter over the hole in the shoe box, it filters out all the colors in white light except for red. When this red light strikes the green gumball, it contains almost no green light for the gumball to reflect, so the gumball looks black. The same is true for the blue gumball. You can't even tell the difference between green and blue. Almost all the light that strikes the red gumball gets reflected. Someone who looks in your red-filtered box containing a red and a blue gumball and tells you what colors they are, will probably say they are white and black. This is because we see objects that reflect a lot of light as white and objects that absorb light as black.

MIXING LIGHT

Materials & Equipment
- red, green, and blue cellophane
- tape or rubber bands

- 3 identical focusable flashlights (see page 91 for a description)
- white paper

Procedure

Fold each piece of cellophane so that it is four layers thick. This will give a deep filtering effect. Put red cellophane over one flashlight, green over another, and blue over the third. Hold the cellophane in place with the tape or rubber bands. For this experiment, unfocus the light to create a broad, even field of illumination.

Shine the red and green lights on the white paper so that their fields mix. Red and green light produce yellow. You can make the red or green light more intense by moving it closer to the paper. Now overlap the blue and green lights and see what color they produce. Try red and blue lights. Finally, overlap all three lights on the white paper. You should see whitish light. You may have to adjust the distances of the lights to the screen so that equal amounts of red, blue, and green light fall on the paper to produce this effect.

Here's What's Happening

Every object or colored light is a mix of more than one color, but the color that you see is called the *dominant* color. When the red light is shining on the paper, the dominant color is in the red part of the spectrum. When the green light is added to it, the dominant color changes. The color you see depends on two things: how bright each is and the sensitivity of the human eye to each. When the red and green lights are of equal brightness, the dominant color is yellow, which is closer in the spectrum to green than it is to red (remember ROY G. BIV). We see yellow, rather than orange, because the human eye is more sensitive to green light than it is to red. By changing the distance of one of the flashlights to the paper, you change the amount of energy that that color is adding to the mixture. Red, green, and blue light are called the *primary colors of light* because all the other colors of the visible spectrum can be created by combining different amounts of these primaries. When you combine equal amounts of red, green, and blue light, white light is created.

The shades of color that you see are not just due to the light source and the amount of light the object reflects. The sensitivity of your eyes to color also plays a big part. (New fire engines are now painted a yellowish green because that is more attention-getting than red.) If an object reflects a tiny amount of red light, a small amount of green light, and a lot of blue light, the dominant color will be blue because the energy of the blue light is much greater than the energy of any other light. However, since your eye more easily detects green light than light of any other color, it takes less energy for green light to be a dominant color than it does for blue or red light.

COLOR WHEEL

Another way to mix colored light is to fool your eyes. If you see two or more colors in rapid alternation, your brain does the mixing. Is the effect the same as actually mixing colored lights? Do the next experiment and find out.

Materials & Equipment
- a small saucer
- white paper
- a pencil
- a ruler
- scissors
- rubber cement
- cardboard
- assorted colored markers or crayons
- a hand-held electric mixer *(check with an adult before you use it)*

Procedure
With the pencil, trace around the saucer on the paper. Use the ruler and pencil to draw lines that will divide the circle into six approximately

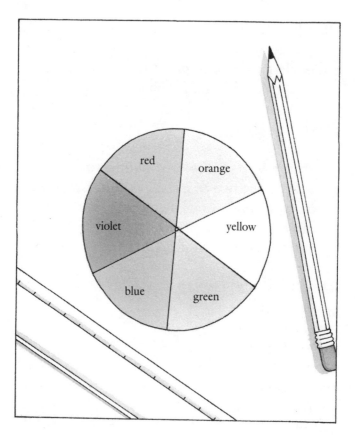

equal pie pieces. Color the pie pieces in the order of the spectrum: one each of red, orange, yellow, green, blue, and violet. Cut out the circle and paste it on the cardboard. Cut out the cardboard, making a stiff color wheel. Poke one beater shaft through the center of the color wheel. Do not insert the second beater into the base. Turn on the mixer to spin the color wheel. Watch the wheel and see what color it appears to be.

Make another wheel, but this time color half the wheel red and the other half green. What color do you see when you spin this one? Experiment with other combinations of colors.

Here's What's Happening

The wheel is made up of the main colors in white light. When the wheel spins fast enough, your brain cannot see the individual colors, and they all fuse together. In this case, you are still looking at colored light, although the source is reflected light instead of actual light as it was in the last experiment. Since each color of white light is present, when they fuse, the wheel appears white.

When the wheel has only two colors, you see what happens when they fuse. For example, red and green again produce yellow. This type of light adding is very similar to projecting different colors on a white piece of paper.

COLOR TELEVISION AND COLOR PRINT

Originally, mass communications media—print and television—were only in black and white. But color is so much more fun. Modern technology uses three colors plus black to fool our eyes into seeing a many-colored media world. How? See for yourself in this next experiment.

Materials & Equipment

- a color TV
- a magnifying glass or pocket microscope
- a magazine

Procedure

Look at the television close-up with the magnifying glass. See what colors actually make a yellow dress or a blue house or someone's white shirt. If you can get hold of a 30x (30-times magnification) pocket microscope (check in a toy store or in a store that sells science experiment materials), the effect of the combination dots will really jump out at you.

Now look at the full-color pictures in a magazine with the magnifier. The colors are made by a similar process; however, it is more difficult to see the dots on the page than on the TV. The pocket microscope reveals them more clearly.

Here's What's Happening

Images in both color television and color printing are made up of thousands of tiny colored dots that are too small for the naked eye to see as dots. A television screen is divided into hundreds of horizontal rows of tiny dots called *pixels*. Each pixel contains a red light, a green light, and a blue light. When the brightness of the lights in each pixel is varied, many different colors and shades can be made. A blue area can be created, for example, if all the pixels in one area receive an increase in brightness of blue light, while the red and green lights are dimmed. Black is created when all the colors in the pixel get dimmed. White is created by turning up all the colors in the pixels. Big-screen TVs have about the same number of pixels as smaller screens, but the pixels are bigger. If you stand close to a big-screen TV, you can easily see the pixels, along with a much fuzzier image.

Mixing color pigments is different from mixing light. When colored lights are mixed, as in the previous experiment, the different colors are *added* together to produce a new color. When different shades of paint are mixed, however, the resulting color is due to a *subtraction* of absorbed light, rather than the addition of different-colored light. Each pigment has a range of colors that it absorbs. For example, blue paint reflects mostly blue light, but also violet and green; it absorbs red, orange, and yellow light. Yellow paint reflects mostly yellow light, but also red, orange, and green; it absorbs blue and violet light. When blue and yellow paint are mixed, between them they absorb all the colors except green, which is the only color they both reflect. The primary colors for pigment mixing are different from those for light mixing, namely: red, yellow, and blue. When you mix the three primary colors, you produce a muddy brown, which is about as close to black (absorption of all wavelengths) as you can get.

Color printing uses three primaries—magenta (purplish red), yellow, and cyan (bluish green)—and black. Each color is printed as tiny separate dots. The size and density of the dots determines the shade of color you see in the finished work. Black is printed after all the other colors.

CLEAR GLASS THAT LIGHT CANNOT GET THROUGH

Transparent materials can also have color. They absorb all wavelengths except those of the color that they *transmit*. (Opaque objects absorb all wavelengths except those of the color they *reflect*.)

Materials & Equipment
- a flashlight
- a glass coffee table whose glass edge is exposed
- a friend
- cellophane of several different colors

Procedure
Have your friend shine the flashlight into the edge of the coffee table while you look at the light through the opposite edge. What color is the light? Experiment with shining light through the coffee table using different-colored cello-

phane filters. Which color makes it through the glass best?

Here's What's Happening

Glass that is used to make coffee tables is sometimes called "green glass" because the edges of it are green. This type of glass absorbs more blue light and red light than it does green light. The light from the flashlight travels through so much glass that by the time it comes out the other end, most of the blue and red light has been absorbed, and the light appears green. This checks out nicely when you try sending red, blue, and green lights through the glass. Most coffee tables and windows are made of green glass. Lenses for optical instruments are made of a high-quality glass that transmits most of the spectrum. If you made a coffee table out of optical glass, the end would appear clear, not green. It would also require more green (money) than most people would want to spend!

"WHITER THAN WHITE" SOAP

Some laundry detergents claim they can get your clothes "whiter than white." This experiment will show you if there is truth to this claim.

Materials & Equipment
• several brands of powdered laundry detergent

(get some that say they really brighten and whiten your wash)
- various white powders (baking soda, flour, salt, ordinary soap flakes, etc.)
- several small dishes
- a black-light bulb (from a novelty or hobby store)

Procedure

Put some of each white powder and each laundry detergent into separate dishes. In a dark room, shine the black light on each dish. See which powders look particularly white and bright under the black light.

Here's What's Happening

A black-light bulb emits a type of light called *ultraviolet*, which you cannot see—it is outside the visible spectrum. A black-light bulb also emits some visible light (mostly violet and blue). There are some chemicals that absorb ultraviolet light and then emit visible light. These chemicals are called *fluorescent* materials. Some detergents contains such materials. If these chemicals remain in your clothes after they are washed, there will be an effect: Sunlight also contains ultraviolet light as well as visible light, and so the ultraviolet light in daylight can make these chemicals give off an increased amount of visible light, making the clothes appear slightly brighter.

Fluorescent light bulbs also use fluorescent materials. Here's how they work: The inside of a fluorescent light bulb is painted with a fluorescent material and filled with mercury vapor. When electricity passes through the mercury vapor, ultraviolet light is emitted. The ultraviolet light strikes the fluorescent material, which then emits the visible white light you see.

Fluorescent lights have several advantages over ordinary incandescent light bulbs. Incandescent lights are much hotter because they produce light by heating a wire until it is white hot. Fluorescent lighting is relatively cool and uses much less electricity than incandescent lamps. However, many people prefer the softer, warmer light of incandescent bulbs.

Some funky colors on clothes really seem to jump out at you. They've been used on ski suits, beach clothes, and running outfits. These "Day-Glo" colors contain dyes that have fluorescent chemicals in them. They actually do radiate more light than normal colors do, by converting invisible ultraviolet light into visible light.

LASERS

Most of the colors that you see are not just a single color (that is, a single wavelength), but a mixture of colors. In 1960 scientists discovered a way to produce an extraordinary colored light that was composed almost exclusively of a single wavelength. They gave the instrument that produced this light the name LASER, which is an acronym for Light Amplification by Stimulated Emission of Radiation. (The acronym quickly came into the language without its capital letters.) It's not quite as complicated as its name might suggest.

A laser has a tube or rod that contains a laser medium. This medium can be a gas or mixture of gasses (such as helium and neon), a crystal (such as a ruby), or a liquid. There is a mirror on each end of the laser tube, and there is also some way of supplying power to the laser.

The power causes the atoms in the medium to become stimulated (excited with energy). Atoms can be excited only for an extremely short time, after which they lose their extra energy by giving off light. This light bounces back and forth between the mirrors. Atoms that have emitted light get excited again and emit more light that reflects back and forth. The light inside the laser tube gets stronger and stronger, acquiring energy from excited atoms. One of the mirrors is constructed to allow some of this light to pass through it. The emerging beam of light is extremely intense. It is all one wavelength (the particular wavelength depends on the laser's medium), and it doesn't spread out very much as it travels over a long distance.

Lasers are used today in some surgery in place of scalpels, to play compact discs, and to automatically read labels of food items with a grocery store scanner, among other things. They are also used to make the holograms on credit cards (See page 146).

UNSEEN COLORS

Visible light is only a small part of a much larger spectrum known as the *electromagnetic spectrum*. Ultraviolet waves, which make skin tan, are invisible. They have a wavelength shorter than the violet end of visible light. Next to ultraviolet are *X rays* and *gamma rays*. Both are very penetrating. Photographs using X rays reveal your bones and cavities in your teeth. Gamma rays are given off during an atom-bomb explosion and are hazardous to your health because they are even more penetrating than X rays. At the other end of the spectrum is invisible light with a longer wavelength than red, called *infrared* light. Infrared light, you remember, is used in your remote control to turn on TVs and VCRs. Infrared radiation in sunlight produces heat. *Microwaves* are even longer than infrared rays. Microwaves can spin water molecules around so fast that they get hot enough to bake a potato in minutes. The longest wavelengths are *radio waves*, which carry radio and television signals through the air to your

The Electromagnetic Spectrum

cosmic rays

gamma rays

X rays

ultraviolet light

visible light ———

infrared light

microwaves

radio waves

10^{10} 10^{9} 10^{8} 10^{7} 10^{6} 10^{5} 10^{4} 10^{3} 10^{2} 10^{1} 1 10^{-1} 10^{-2} 10^{-3} 10^{-4} 10^{-5} 10^{-6} 10^{-7} 10^{-8} 10^{-9} 10^{-10}

Wavelength is measured in microns (one micron = one millionth of a meter).

10^{10} microns = 10 kilometers, or about 6 miles

If you could split a hair from your head into 5,000 equal slices, one slice would be 10^{-1} microns.

10^{-10} microns is one billion times smaller than that.

radio and TV antennas. They also give us fascinating information about the universe. Radio
telescopes are enormous dishes that act as curved
mirrors to collect radio waves from distant galax-
ies and focus them on a central receiver so that
scientists can study them.

Chapter Nine

MAKING WAVES

Water waves can be used as a model for understanding the behavior of light waves. A water wave is a pulse of energy moving through water. It has a high point, called the *crest* and a low point, called the *trough*. The distance from crest to crest is identical to the distance from trough to trough and is known as the *wavelength*.

Scientists have traditionally studied waves with a device called a "ripple tank." Using the swimming-pool effect (discussed in Chapter 4), experimenters shine light onto a glass surface through water waves that are generated in shallow water. They project an image of the waves onto a white screen. It is the job of a research scientist to come up with questions and then to design ways to get answers. A ripple tank gives scientists a way to get answers to questions such as these:

What happens to the wavelength when waves are generated faster and faster? What happens to a wave after it encounters an obstacle? Does the size of the obstacle make a difference? What happens to a wave after it passes through an opening? Does the size of the opening matter? What happens to a wave when it catches up to another wave? What happens to a wave when it crosses another wave?

In this chapter we use a ripple tank to understand two unusual light phenomena: *interference*, which causes, among other things, the colors in a soap bubble or an oil film; and *diffraction*, which creates colors on a compact disc or a vinyl record.

There's more than one way to make a ripple tank. We'll tell you how we made ours, but feel free to improvise.

THE RIPPLE TANK

Materials & Equipment
- books (to act as props that elevate the tank)
- a 10" x 15" x 2" clear glass baking dish
- water
- a white countertop or a piece of white paper
- a flashlight
- aluminum foil
- a pencil
- an eyedropper or a straw

- a pencil, dowel, or other long, narrow cylindrical object that can get wet
- a ruler

Procedure

Stack books on a table or countertop to make two piles about eight inches high each. Separate the piles so that you can rest either end of the glass baking dish securely on a stack of books. Pour water into the dish to a depth of one inch. Check the water from the side and make adjustments (by adding or subtracting books) so that the dish is level and the water is at the same depth everywhere in the dish. If your table isn't

white, place the white paper on the table below the dish. Cover the head of the flashlight with aluminum foil so that no light can get out. Poke a small hole in the middle of the foil with the pencil to make a small light source. Your ripple tank is now ready to ripple.

Turn out all other lights, and hold the lit flashlight two feet over the ripple tank. Use the eyedropper to drip a single drop of water into the center of the dish. (If you don't have an eyedropper, you can use a straw. Put one end of the straw in the water and then place your finger over the other end to create a tight seal. Take the straw out of the water. When you release your finger from the end of the straw, the water drips into the tank.) Watch the white surface under the ripple tank from below the tank, not through the

water. You should see wave shadows as you drip drops into the water. Generate waves with drips at one end of the ripple tank. They will begin as semicircular waves, but by the time they get to the other side of the tank they should be almost straight lines. You can imagine that if the ripple tank were long enough, there would be a point where the waves would be straight lines. To understand diffraction, it helps to have straight-line waves.

You can generate straight-line waves in a ripple tank with a pencil that is floating at one end of the tank. Gently tap its center downward with another pencil or your finger. You might also try generating regular straight-line waves with a ruler. Hold the ruler so it is resting on the bottom of the dish on one long edge. Move the top edge back and forth to produce waves. You see the wavelength of these water waves, the distance from one crest to another, as the distance between one bright line on the screen and the next. Once you've mastered generating regular straight-line waves, you're ready to do the next two experiments.

DIFFRACTION BETWEEN WAX BLOCKS

Materials & Equipment
• wax blocks (from a hardware or housewares

store; used to make candles or for canning)
- a knife
- the ripple tank from the last experiment
- a pencil or dowel, or a six-inch ruler, to create straight-line waves

Procedure

Cut a wedge shape from one end of each of two wax blocks. Place the blocks in the tank to make a barrier with the wedged ends forming an opening of about one-quarter inch. The barrier should be about four inches from the end of the tank where the pencil or ruler is. Generate straight-line waves. Watch the screen to see what happens to the waves as they go through the opening. The waves emerge from the opening with a semicircular shape. Change the size of the opening by moving the blocks closer and farther apart and see what effect this has on the emerging waves.

Here's What's Happening

When the opening between the wax blocks is about the same size as or smaller than the wavelength, you can see how the wave *diffracts* through the opening.

Diffraction is the bending of a wave around an obstacle. The waves that emerge from the narrow opening are semicircular and very similar to the waves made by the eyedropper. As the opening

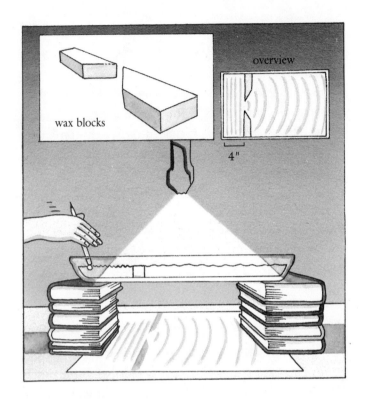

overview

wax blocks

4"

between the wax blocks get larger, the diffraction of the wave becomes less obvious. In the next experiment you will use diffraction to create two circular wave sources to see interference.

INTERFERENCE IN A RIPPLE TANK

Materials & Equipment
- all materials from previous experiment
- another wax block

Procedure

Cut a piece of wax to make a block that is one inch long. Cut the corners to make a wedge on each end. Move the two wax blocks from the previous experiment so they are about 1½ inches apart. Then place this block in between. This will create a barrier with two quarter-inch openings that are about one inch apart. Again, the barrier should be about four inches from the end of the ripple tank where the waves are generated. Generate waves and watch the screen to see how they diffract through both openings. Look for dark lines that are perpendicular to the waves; they may be difficult to see.

Here's What's Happening

When the straight-line waves diffract through the two openings, two sources of semicircular waves are created. When the crest of a wave from one opening meets the trough of a wave from the other opening, they cancel each other out, producing a dark spot on the screen. When a crest of a wave from one opening meets the crest of a wave from the other opening, they add together to make a bigger crest, producing a bright spot. When there are lots of waves from two sources, there are lots of crest-trough and crest-crest meetings, producing dark and light patterns called *interference bands* or *fringes*.

We demonstrated diffraction in our ripple tank

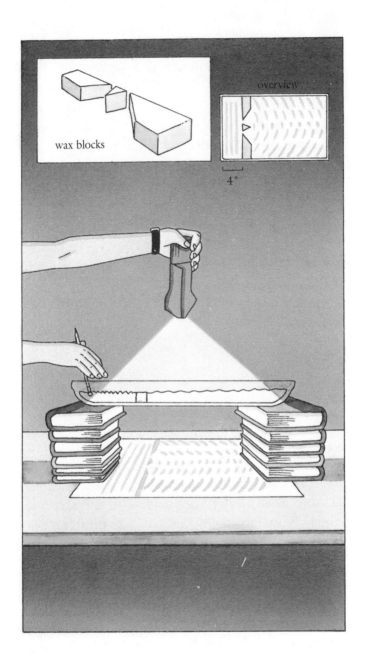

wax blocks

overview

4"

because it is an easy way to produce two sources of identical waves, and identical waves work best for showing the way waves interfere with one another. Interference patterns between waves can happen no matter how the waves are generated. Here are several experiments that will let you see what happens when light waves interfere with one another.

BUBBLE FILMS

Materials & Equipment
- liquid dishwashing soap
- a small bowl
- a straw
- warm water
- a lamp

Procedure
Put three tablespoons of liquid dishwashing soap in the bowl. Slowly pour in two cups of warm water and mix with the straw. Try to keep foam from forming on the surface of the liquid. Set the bowl under the lamp. Use the straw to slowly blow into the liquid to make bubbles. You need to make a large bubble. To do this, get a bubble started that is connected to the sides of the bowl. Then gently draw the end of the straw out of the liquid while keeping it inside the bubble. Continue to blow gently. Watch the surface

of the bubble that is over the reflection of the lamp. Notice the changing colors. When the bubble is about two inches high, stop blowing. Watch the lamp's reflection and watch the surface of the bubble. In addition to seeing swirling colors moving across the reflection, you will see black spots on the surface. The black areas increase right before the bubble bursts. In fact, the appearance of black can predict that bursting is imminent.

Here's What's Happening

A bubble is a very thin transparent film of liquid with two surfaces. When light strikes a bubble, some of it reflects off the outside surface of the film and some of it passes through until it strikes the inside surface. The inside surface also reflects some light and passes some light through to the inside of the bubble. The reflection off both surfaces creates two sources of light waves, just as you had two sources of waves in the ripple tank. The waves from these sources interfere with each other in much the same way your ripple tank waves interfered with each other. *Constructive interference* shows up as a bright color, as the crests of that color's waves add together. The color of the light depends on the thickness of the bubble. A thicker film produces red, which has the longer wavelength; a thinner film produces blue. So the colors on a bubble's surface

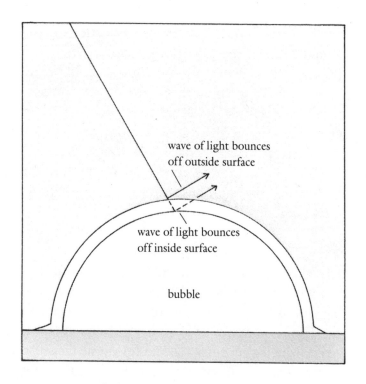

wave of light bounces
off outside surface

wave of light bounces
off inside surface

bubble

are a map of the varying thicknesses of the bubble film. When the film thins to a quarter of the wavelength of light (about one ten-thousandth of a millimeter, or four ten-thousandths of an inch) all the light waves interfere *destructively* (troughs meet crests) and they cancel each other out, producing black spots. This is about as thin as the film can get. So the sudden increase in black on the surface indicates that the film is quickly becoming too thin for the bubble to support itself. The bubble bursts.

The distances we are talking about are extremely small. If you could split a hair from your head into five thousand equal slices, one slice would be one ten-thousandth of a millimeter thick.

OIL SLICKS

Like bubbles, oil on wet roads and parking lots produces colored patterns created by the interference of light waves. Motor oil leaked from cars forms a thin film on the surface of the water. Light reflects off the top and bottom surfaces of the oil. The varying thickness of the oil film determines which colors are produced, just as the thicknesses of the bubble film produce a variety of colors.

COLORS IN CLEAR ACETATE

Materials & Equipment
- two pieces of acetate (from an art supply or stationery store)
- black construction paper
- a coin
- a lamp

Procedure
Put the two pieces of acetate together and place them on top of the black construction paper under the lamp. Find the reflection of the

141

lamp in the acetate and watch it as you do the experiment. Rub the edge of the coin in one direction along the top sheet of acetate, pressing down hard. Repeat the motion. Watch for colors in the acetate and see how they change when you stop rubbing.

Here's What's Happening

The two pieces of acetate are separated by a thin air pocket. Light reflects off the bottom surface of the top sheet and the top surface of the bottom sheet, and the waves interfere. When the two sheets are just lying together, the air gap between them is too large for interference to occur. By pressing the coin on the acetate, you can squeeze out the air in some sections and make the air gap small enough for interference to occur. The different thicknesses of the air gaps cause interference bands or fringes of different wavelengths, and you see changing colors. The black paper blocks extra reflections so you can see the interference fringes more clearly.

A POCKET COMB WITH FALSE TEETH

Materials & Equipment
- a pocket comb
- a wall mirror

Procedure

Face the mirror. Hold the comb at eye level about half an inch from the mirror with the teeth facing up. Look at the reflection of your eyes through the comb and slowly move the comb back and forth, parallel to the mirror. You should see dark bands or thicker "teeth" in the comb. The number of thicker bands changes depending on the distance between the comb and the mirror.

Here's What's Happening

The teeth of a comb create bands of light and darkness. The teeth block light, and the spaces between the teeth pass light. The comb you see in the mirror appears slightly smaller than the comb you are holding because the image is farther away from your eyes. Thus, the spacing between the teeth in the reflection appears slightly smaller than the spacing of the actual comb. This slight difference in the spacing affects the way the light and dark areas line up when the comb moves. Sometimes the blocked areas appear bunched together, creating wider dark bands surrounded by light areas. These larger dark bands and surrounding lighter areas are a different kind of interference called a *moiré pattern*. You can see moiré patterns when one piece of wire screen is moved at an angle over another. Moiré silk is a kind of fabric with ridges that reflect light in changing moiré patterns. Sometimes a small plaid or stripe pattern in the clothing of someone on television will produce a moiré pattern through interference with the scanning lines of the TV screen.

FEATHER FRINGES

Materials & Equipment
- a feather with interlocking barbs, such as a goose feather
- a light source

Procedure
Hold the feather close to your eye, spreading the barbs just enough so that you can see light through the feather. Look at a light source through the feather. *(Caution: Never look directly at the sun.)* The spectrum appears. Which color is farthest from the light and which is closest?

Here's What's Happening
The ripple tank shows that diffraction is the transformation of a wave front as it passes through a small opening. The emerging wave bends around the edges of the opening. Like the waves in your ripple tank, light waves are diffracted when they pass through small openings.

The interior of the vane (the flat part) of a feather has many spaces small enough to diffract light. The amount of diffraction depends on the wavelength or color of the light and the size of the opening it passes through. When white light passes through a tiny opening, the different colors in the light spread out in different amounts. The red light waves that spread out as they pass through one opening interfere with red light waves that are spread out by all the other openings. The same thing happens with all the other colors. The spreading of the different wavelengths and the interference of all the colors produce colored fringes.

Scientists use an instrument that does the same thing to light as the feather does. It's called a *diffraction grating*. Tightly spaced parallel lines are scratched on a piece of glass with a diamond point. The spaces between these lines diffract light as the vane of a feather does. Light that passes through a diffraction grating is separated into its spectrum. Light from heavenly bodies is analyzed this way. The spectrum of a particular star gives information about its temperature and the elements that are present in it. The particular wavelengths that are present and the width of each band are like fingerprints for each star.

COLORFUL COMPACT DISCS

Materials & Equipment
- a compact disc (commonly called a "CD")

- several different light sources

Procedure

Hold the CD at an angle to a light source and look at the spectrum that is reflected. Closely examine the colors of that light's spectrum. Try looking for different kinds of light sources such as streetlamps, fluorescent lamps, black lights, candles, and anything else you can think of.

Here's What's Happening

A compact disc is a kind of diffraction grating. If you were to look at a magnified image of the CD's surface, you would see countless tiny pits with spaces between them. When ordinary white light hits the CD, the light diffracts off the edges of the pits, and the colored lights spread out. Different light sources produce different colors of light. For example, an incandescent light bulb has more yellow in it than a fluorescent bulb. A compact disc will show different colors depending on the wavelengths present in the light you shine on it.

HOLOGRAMS

Materials & Equipment

- a credit card with a hologram (three-dimensional picture) on it

Procedure

Look at the hologram on the credit card from different angles. Notice its three-dimensional appearance.

Here's What's Happening

Holograms are special photographs made with lasers. The photographs work on the principles of diffraction and interference. Very realistic holograms, called *transmission holograms*, not only are made with lasers but also can only be seen using a laser. Transmission holograms are used to make the *white-light holograms* that are on credit cards. It is necessary to understand a transmission hologram before you can understand a white-light hologram.

Here's how a transmission hologram is made: A laser beam is split into two beams. Lenses enlarge both beams so that they spread over a wider area. One beam (the *object beam*) strikes the object that is to be the "picture" in the hologram. When this light reflects off the object, it lands on a glass plate. The other beam (the *reference beam*) strikes the glass without striking the object. When both beams hit the glass, they interfere with each other to form a weird fringe pattern. The glass has a photographic emulsion on it and exactly records the fringe pattern. When the glass is developed (just as any other

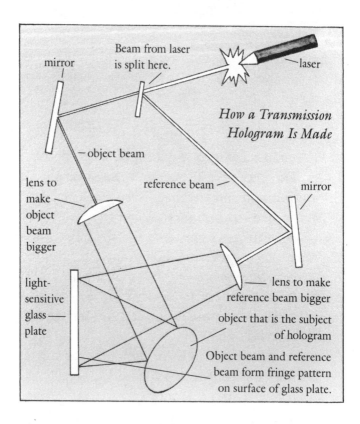

How a Transmission Hologram Is Made

- mirror
- Beam from laser is split here.
- laser
- object beam
- reference beam
- mirror
- lens to make object beam bigger
- light-sensitive glass plate
- lens to make reference beam bigger
- object that is the subject of hologram
- Object beam and reference beam form fringe pattern on surface of glass plate.

photograph is developed), all you can see are interference fringes.

Here's how the hologram is viewed: The glass with the fringes is returned to the spot where the two beams hit it. The object is removed, and the glass plate is illuminated only by a reference beam. The reference beam directly strikes the glass, where it diffracts around the recorded fringes. This restores the same light waves that actually reflected off the object. You see a reconstructed

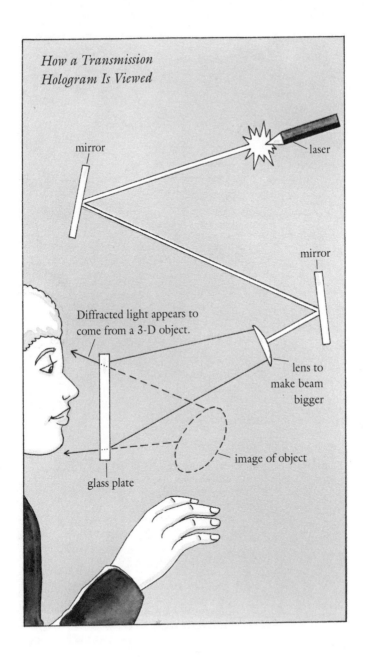

How a Transmission Hologram Is Viewed

mirror

laser

mirror

Diffracted light appears to come from a 3-D object.

lens to make beam bigger

image of object

glass plate

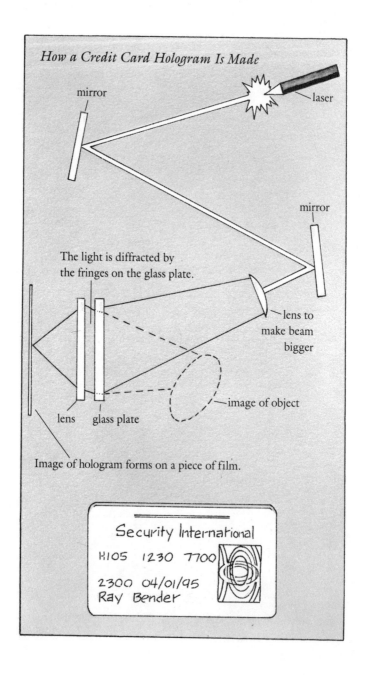

How a Credit Card Hologram Is Made

mirror

laser

mirror

The light is diffracted by
the fringes on the glass plate.

lens to
make beam
bigger

image of object

lens   glass plate

Image of hologram forms on a piece of film.

Security International

H105 1230 7700

2300 04/01/95
Ray Bender

image of the object, in three dimensions, at the original location of the object. If a second holographic image is recorded on the same glass plate at a slightly different angle, then you see two views of the object when you change your viewing angle. Two-image holograms can produce an illusion of motion: a runner with moving legs or a face breaking into a smile.

A white-light hologram on a credit card is made by using a lens to focus an image of a transmission hologram onto photographic film. This is done in a fashion very similar to the way you formed an image of the TV on the piece of paper. When the film is developed, the white-light hologram is produced. Since holograms are very hard to reproduce, they are a protection against counterfeiting.

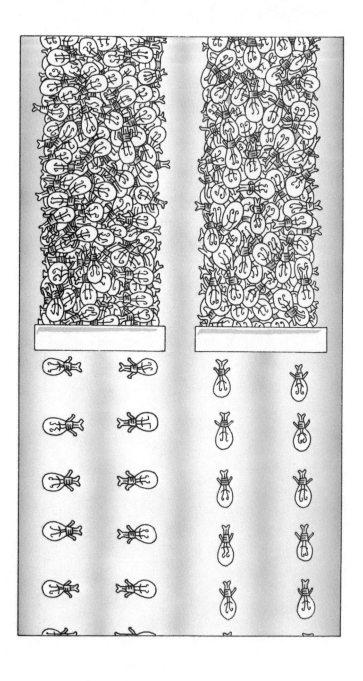

·

Chapter Ten

POLARIZED LIGHT

What advantage do polarized sunglasses have over ordinary sunglasses? The answer is glaringly obvious (that's a little "light" humor). They reduce glare. Nonpolarized sunglasses are designed just to block light. Polarized sunglasses block light also, but they also block glare, which is polarized light. In this chapter, you'll discover what polarized light is and how polarized lenses work. Polarized lenses can be used to see some pretty unusual phenomena.

The next experiment is a good model for helping you to understand polarized light.

THE MOVING ROPE AND THE GATE

Materials & Equipment
- a 25-foot piece of clothesline
- 2 broomsticks, 2 skis, or 2 long boards
- a friend

Procedure

Find a long distance (such as a hallway) with a door at the end of it. Tie one end of the clothesline to the doorknob and go to the other end of the hall. Hold the line in one hand and move it vigorously up and down. You should be able to make some waves travel down the line. Now move the rope from side to side to make waves that travel horizontally down the line. Have a friend stand in the middle of the hallway. Have your friend hold each broomstick vertically to make a two-inch "gate" that the line goes through. Make vertical waves and notice that they pass through the gate unaltered. What happens when you generate horizontal waves? It is not surprising that the gate stops the waves that are at right angles to the opening. Now swing your arm in a large circle to produce circular waves. Notice the direction of the waves that emerge from the far side of the gate. They are all vertical. The gate has effectively blocked the horizontal component. Now try swinging your arm every which way to produce waves in random directions. What kind of waves come out of the gate? Order emerges from chaos.

Here's What's Happening

The waves of ordinary light vibrate in all directions, like the rope in the last part of the experiment. The purpose of the gate is to separate

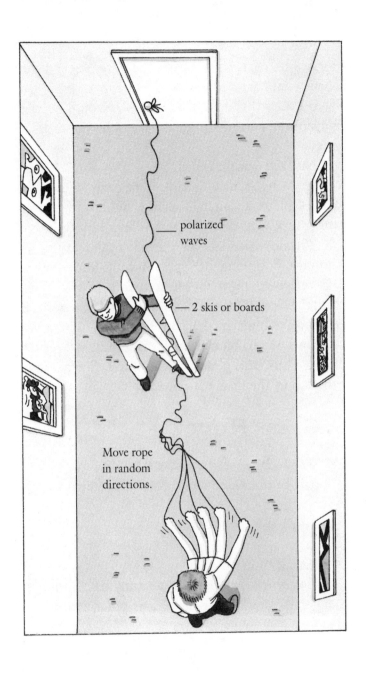

the waves into two parts, a vertical part and a horizontal part. In this case, the gate blocked the horizontal part and let the vertical part through. If you turned the gate sideways, it would let the horizontal part through and block the vertical part.

Polarized sunglasses act like the gate. When ordinary light is vibrating randomly, the sunglasses block about half of the light, and things don't appear to be so bright. When light bounces off certain materials at certain angles (such as sunlight bouncing off car windows and roads), the reflected light vibrates mainly in the horizontal plane. This reflected light, which you see as glare, is polarized light. Polarized sunglasses are designed to block most horizontally vibrating light. Thus, the glare is eliminated. See this for yourself in the next experiment.

A GLARE HUNT

Materials & Equipment
- a pair of polarized sunglasses (most drugstores have them)
- a sunny day

Procedure
It's easy to find glare on a sunny day. Sunlight that reflects off water or glass is polarized. Look

at a glaring car windshield without your glasses. If the glare is strong enough, you will not be able to see through the windshield. Keep looking while you put your glasses on. The polarizers should let you see right through the glare and into the car. Keep looking for glare with and without your glasses. Tilt your head sideways. See how the glare disappears and reappears as you change your viewing angle.

Here's What's Happening

Tilting your head with your sunglasses on is like turning the gate sideways. Horizontally polarized light can pass through the glasses and vertically polarized light gets blocked. If you're lying sideways at the beach, your glasses won't block the glare off the water.

Fishermen very often use polarized sunglasses because this helps them to see underneath the surface of a lake or stream. The polarized sunglasses allow them to spot fish under the water.

BLOCK LIGHT WITH A PIECE OF TRANSPARENT TAPE

Materials & Equipment
- 2 pairs of polarized sunglasses
- transparent cellophane tape (the older it is, the better)

Procedure

Put on one pair of sunglasses and hold the other pair up to a light. Look at the light through both pairs of glasses. Rotate the glasses you are holding. Notice that the lenses change from light to dark and back again.

Now take a piece of tape and stick it across one of the polarized lenses. While wearing the other pair, hold the taped sunglasses up to the light and rotate the glasses again. Notice that when the lens gets dark, the tape gets light. Keep rotating, and this situation reverses.

Now place a second piece of tape across the first to form an X. Again, rotate the lens. A different dark and light pattern forms. Put additional pieces of tape across the lens in many different directions. You can create a crazy pattern.

Here's What's Happening

Light that passes through a polarizer emerges as polarized light. Suppose that light traveling through the first polarizer (in your hand) becomes horizontally polarized. This means that vertically vibrating light is blocked, and the emerging light is vibrating horizontally when it reaches the second polarizer (in front of your eyes). If the second polarizer is oriented so that it blocks horizontally vibrating light and passes only vertically vibrating light, all of the light will

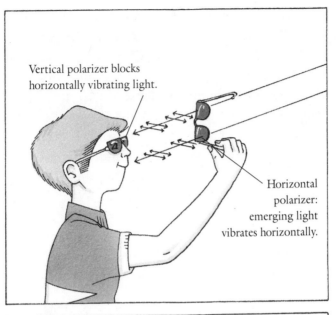

Vertical polarizer blocks horizontally vibrating light.

Horizontal polarizer: emerging light vibrates horizontally.

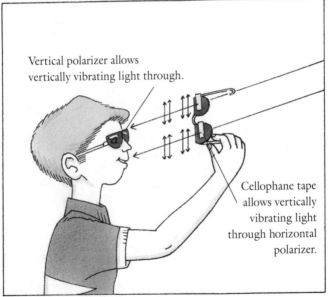

Vertical polarizer allows vertically vibrating light through.

Cellophane tape allows vertically vibrating light through horizontal polarizer.

be blocked. The result is that the lenses appear dark. When you rotate the first polarizer, the orientation slowly changes until it passes light that is vibrating vertically. The vertically vibrating light passes through the lenses in front of your eyes, and the lenses appear light. As you keep rotating one pair of lenses in front of the pair you're wearing, light and dark alternate.

The cellophane has the peculiar ability to flop the orientation of the polarization. When light is vibrating horizontally, it will vibrate vertically after passing through the tape, and vice versa. The appearance of the lens will be opposite the appearance of the tape as one set of polarizers is rotated.

In areas where two pieces of tape cross, the polarization flops twice thus canceling out the effect.

MAKE A RAINBOW APPEAR AND DISAPPEAR

Materials & Equipment
- a garden hose
- a pair of polarized sunglasses
- a sunny day

Procedure
Make a rainbow in your backyard with the garden hose in the same manner described on page

102. Put on polarized sunglasses and look at the rainbow. Part of it disappears. When you tilt your head sideways, you should see it reappear.

Here's What's Happening

The light from the rainbow is polarized. The direction of polarization changes along the bow of the rainbow. As you change the angle of your polarized lenses, parts of the rainbow appear and disappear as light is transmitted and blocked according to the way the light lines up with the lens.

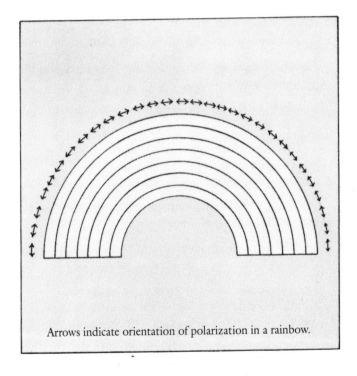

Arrows indicate orientation of polarization in a rainbow.

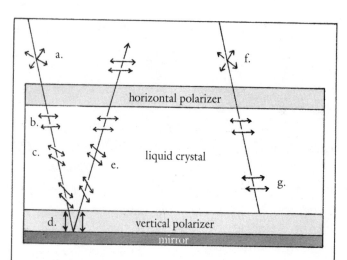

LCD Sandwich

a. Randomly vibrating light enters LCD sandwich.

b. Only horizontally vibrating light gets through the horizontal polarizer.

c. The liquid crystal flops the light so that it is vibrating vertically.

d. The vertical light passes through the vertical polarizer and bounces off the mirror, back through the vertical polarizer, and into the liquid crystal again.

e. The liquid crystal flops the light back to horizontal, so it passes through the horizontal polarizer.

f. Randomly vibrating light enters LCD sandwich. Only horizontally vibrating light gets through.

g. If a voltage is applied to this area, the liquid crystal does not flop horizontal light to vertical, so it is blocked by the vertical polarizer—no light is reflected out.

Sunglasses that Stop Time

Materials & Equipment

- an LCD (liquid crystal display) wristwatch (these are the digital watches that have black numbers; an LCD calculator will also work in place of the watch)
- a pair of polarized sunglasses

Procedure

Hold the watch in your hand and look at the time through the sunglasses. Slowly rotate the watch and the numbers will "magically" disappear. Keep turning and they'll reappear.

Here's What's Happening

Your digital watch or calculator works with a liquid crystal display sandwich. The crystal is sandwiched between two crossed polarizers, and it functions very much like the cellophane tape: It is a polarization flopper. After light from an outside source (daylight, lamplight) passes through the first polarizer, the light vibrates horizontally. The liquid crystal flops the light so that it vibrates vertically. It then passes through the bottom vertical polarizer, reflects off a mirror, and starts its journey back. When it goes through the liquid crystal, the vertically vibrating light flops to horizontally vibrating light, and it gets through the top polarizer again. The

163

face of the watch appears to be light gray all over. However, when a small electric charge passes through the liquid crystal, it loses its flopping ability. When electricity is applied to the liquid crystal, the polarization doesn't flop, and the light never makes it back out of the watch. So wherever there is a charge applied to the liquid crystal, the surface of the watch appears black. Numbers can be displayed by putting a charge over certain parts of the crystal.

Since the top layer of the LCD sandwich has a polarizer on it, you can't see anything in the watch when your polarized glasses are aligned at right angles to the watch's polarizer.

STRESSED-OUT GELATIN

Materials & Equipment
- a 1-inch cube of gelled unflavored gelatin
- two polarized lenses (from your polarized sunglasses)
- a bright light (*not* the sun)

Procedure
Rotate the lenses until the polarizers are crossed and very little light gets through. Sandwich the gelatin between the two polarized lenses. Hold the sandwich up to the light and look through it. Now press on the side of the

gelatin. You should see wavy patterns of darkness in places where the gelatin is being stressed.

Here's What's Happening

In the experiment with the tape, all the polarized light emerging through the tape is flopped the same amount, at right angles to the way it went in. When polarized light passes through gelatin, it is also flopped, but the emerging light is flopped unevenly. Different parts of the gelatin flop the entering polarized light in different amounts. Stressing the gelatin increases the unevenness of the light flopping. This shows up as light being blocked in some areas and not in others. You see bands of dark and light. Different wavelengths are also flopped in different amounts, so you see little fringes of color. This color phenomenon is called *stress birefringence.*

HUNTING FOR STRESS

Materials & Equipment
- two polarized sunglass lenses
- a bright light (*not* the sun)
- plastic wrap
- a clear plastic ruler
- a cassette tape container
- other clear plastic objects

Procedure

Look around the house for clear plastic objects that might exhibit stress birefringence. Sandwich each object between the two crossed polarizers and look for color fringes.

Here's What's Happening

The household plastics that show stress birefringence between two crossed polarizers usually show more brilliant colors than gelatin shows. This is because the stresses within the plastics are more complicated than the stress in the gelatin. The fringes show up like contour lines on a map that link points of equal altitude. A fringe links all the points of equal stress. The areas where the fringes are very close together are the areas of greatest stress.

Stress birefringence is used to study stress on all kinds of materials and structures. For example, scientists can create a model of a skyscraper that is to be built in an earthquake zone. The model is made of a material that becomes birefringent when stress is applied. The scientists simulate the kinds of stresses that the building would experience in an earthquake. The birefringence in the model shows where the stresses are going to be the greatest, so that the actual building can be appropriately reinforced.

THE DEPOLARIZER

Materials & Equipment
- two polarized sunglass lenses
- waxed paper
- a light source (*not* the sun)

Procedure
Put a piece of waxed paper between two polarized lenses so only one half of the lenses are covered. Look at the light source through your "sandwich." Rotate one of the lenses. Notice that the light coming through the waxed-paper side of the sandwich doesn't change its brightness while the other half of the lens alternates light and dark.

Here's What's Happening
As polarized light emerges from one of the lenses and passes through the waxed paper, the particles in the paper scatter the light. This depolarizes the light, so rotating the lens has no effect on the brightness. It's as if you rotated one lens by itself.

LIGHT-FLOPPING SYRUP

Materials & Equipment
- two polarized sunglass lenses

- a clear drinking glass
- a flashlight
- corn syrup
- a friend

Procedure

Put one of the polarized lenses under the bottom of the empty glass and shine the flashlight up through the glass. (You can also use a glass coffee table as a platform and shine the flashlight through the lens, tabletop, and glass from under the table.) Hold the other polarized lens above the glass and look down through both of them at the flashlight. Rotate the top polarizer until the two polarizers are crossed and a minimum amount of light gets through. Hold that position steadily while a friend slowly pours syrup into the glass. Watch the light brighten and change colors as the glass fills with the syrup. When the glass is full, rotate one of the polarizers and again notice the effect this has on the light from the flashlight.

Here's What's Happening

The first polarized lens polarizes the light that enters the syrup. The corn syrup is another light flopper. Its effect on polarized light depends on the depth of the syrup in the glass and on the wavelength (or color) of the light. For a particular depth of syrup, blue light, with a shorter

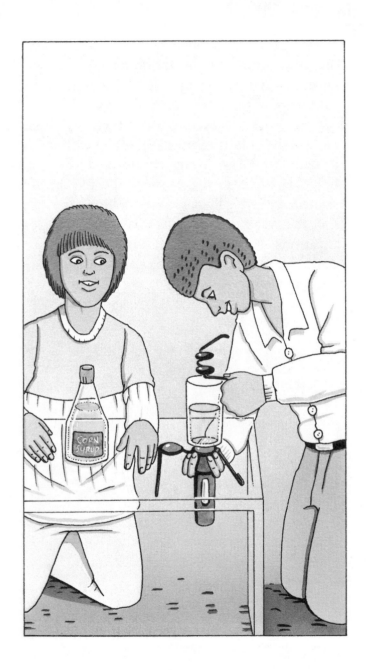

wavelength, gets flopped more than red light. The orientation of polarization changes as light moves through the syrup, but the shorter wavelengths change faster than the longer wavelengths. The second lens passes the color of light that has the polarization that lines up with it. As the depth of the syrup changes, the color that has the polarization to make it through the second lens changes too. By the time the light emerges from the syrup, all the colors have different polarizations. As you rotate the polarizer in your hand, you can block some of them out and pass others through.

Chapter Eleven

CATCHING LIGHT

By now, you should have a pretty good idea that light has some unique properties. It can pass through some materials and can be absorbed by others. It travels at a mind-boggling speed. It can be bent to converge at a point, intensified to perform surgery, and transmitted through space to trigger a switch on a space probe, or to carry the human voice around the world. It breaks up to form a rainbow, it scatters to make the sky blue and sunsets red, and it interferes with itself to create rainbow hues on bubbles and oil films.

A question raised by scientists long ago was: Is light truly something unique or is it a part of something else? The answer did not come to scientists in a blinding flash, but slowly evolved as different scientists contributed bits and pieces that gradually began to fit together like pieces in a jigsaw puzzle. As the puzzle took shape, it took the form of a really big idea, which scientists called *energy*.

At first, some of the pieces seemed to have nothing to do with light. In 1798 Benjamin Thompson, also known as Count Rumford (1753–1814), an English physicist, noticed that heat was generated when cannons were bored. He concluded that the mechanical motion of the boring tool was converted to heat. In 1807 Thomas Young (1773–1829), an English physician and physicist, became the first scientist to formulate the idea of energy as that property of a system or substance that can move matter. In 1849, almost fifty years after Rumford's observations, the English physicist James Joule (1818–1889) actually measured how much mechanical energy (energy of motion) equaled how much heat energy. Every bit of energy in the transformation of motion to heat could be accounted for. No energy was lost. Michael Faraday (1791–1867), an English chemist and physicist, made a connection between electrical energy and chemical energy (the energy that is used to transform molecules from one substance into another) when he passed electric currents through different solutions. He invented the battery, in which a chemical reaction is the source of an electric current. German physicist Julius Mayer (1814–1878) extended the idea that motion and heat were forms of energy and said that energy includes the heat produced by living things, the light from the sun, the heat produced when fuel burns, the motion of the tides, and the heating of meteors as they fall through the atmosphere. He further argued that light from the sun was the source of all energy on earth.

The German physicist Hermann von Helmholtz (1821–1894), considered all of these ideas about energy. He put the pieces together and formulated the law of conservation of energy, which states: Energy cannot be created or destroyed, it can only be transformed from one form to another.

So in spite of its unique properties, light is simply one of many forms of energy. Other forms of energy are heat, electricity, motion, sound, atomic energy, and chemical energy. Light energy that is transformed into other energies is the basis of our vision, photography, fossil fuels, and even life itself. In this chapter we will explore some of the ways light is caught and transformed.

MAKE A GHOST APPEAR ON A WALL

Procedure

Stare at the picture of the ghost on page 176 under a bright light for one minute. Quickly

turn your head and look at a white wall. You should see an image of the ghost on the wall.

Here's What's Happening

You have just become the victim of an after-image. The lens of your eye focuses an image of the ghost on a surface at the back of your eyeball called the *retina,* which comes from a Latin word (*rete*) meaning "net." (The retina is one place in the human body where it is easy to see a network of blood vessels.) The retina contains two types of light-sensitive receptor cells: *rods* and *cones*. Rods are sensitive to dim light, so you can see at night. But they see only poorly defined black-and-white images. The cones are sensitive to color. However, cones need adequate light in order to be used effectively. When light strikes a receptor cell, it initiates a signal in a nerve fiber that conducts the signal to the brain through the optic nerve. The firing of a nerve is a combination of electrical and chemical energy. The brain integrates the electrochemical messages from all the nerves and interprets the messages, translating them back into an image. When you stare at the picture of the ghost, the retinal nerves keep firing over and over until they get overused.

After you stop staring at the picture, the same receptor cells continue to fire. Since signals are still being sent over the optic nerve to the brain, an image is perceived although you are no longer looking at it.

THE BLIND SPOT

Your optic nerve is a vital part of the optical system in your eyes, but it also prevents you from seeing certain things. Do the next experiment to find out why.

Procedure

Put your hand over your left eye and look with your right eye at the boy in the picture on page 178. Slowly move the book closer to and away from your face. You should find a region where the boy's ball disappears. Try this again, covering your right eye and looking with your left eye.

Here's What's Happening

There is a spot on your retina where you can't catch any light. This is the small area where your optic nerve attaches to the back of your eye. When you focus on the boy, his ball is focused on a different part of your retina. By moving the

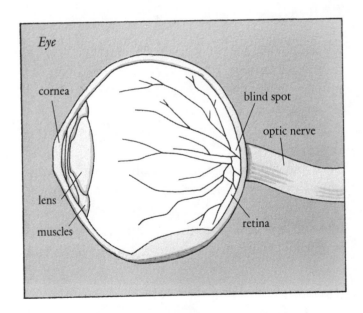

book and keeping your eye focused on the boy, you move the image of the ball around on your retina. When the image goes across the blind spot of your eye, it disappears.

Catch Light on a Silver Tray

Materials & Equipment
- a silver or silver-plated tray
- silver polish
- iodine solution from a pharmacy *(Caution: Iodine is poisonous, and it stains.)*
- a flat, opaque object such as a key (Note: Don't use a silver object, as it will be tarnished by the iodine.)
- a lamp

Procedure
Ask permission to use the silver tray. You can polish it after you're finished, and no harm will be done to it.

Polish the tray with the silver polish until it is very shiny. Notice the brown color of the iodine. Turn out the lights and carefully pour the iodine onto the tray until it completely covers its surface. While still in the dark, pour off the excess iodine into the sink and place the key on the tray while it is still wet. Turn on the lamp and shine it directly onto the tray for two minutes. When you lift up the key, you should see a silhouette on the tray where the key used to be. The image will fade away quickly as more light shines on that area.

Here's What's Happening

The light causes the silver and the brown iodine to combine in a chemical reaction to form a new substance, called silver iodide, which is dark, not silvery or brown. This is called a *photochemical reaction* because it involves both light (*photo* in Greek means "light") and chemistry. The area under the key doesn't get exposed to the light, so it remains silvery. When you remove the key, the light strikes that area, and the photochemical reaction occurs, erasing the silhouette.

Photography is possible because of photochemistry. For black-and-white photos, a camera lens focuses an image on film that has a coating that reacts when light strikes it. The light from the image produces a pattern of chemical change on the film. Later, in a darkroom, the film is put through a series of chemical reactions that makes the light-dark pattern visible and fixes it so that it is permanent. The developed film is a negative. In a negative, the darker areas of the image are light and the lighter areas are dark. Prints are made from the negatives on light-sensitive paper. After development, the light and dark areas on the print show up as they were in the original image.

SEARCHING FOR ELECTRIC EYES

Electric eyes are used for everything from stopping a conveyor belt in the supermarket to detecting burglars in action. They transform light into electrical energy. See how many different kinds of electric eyes you can find in your town. Here are some clues to help you get started.

Elevator Door Openers

When elevators were first invented, someone had to think of a way to open the door when it began closing on someone. Older elevators use a mechanical device in which a rubber-covered edge gets depressed when it comes in contact with a person. The force of the depression triggers a mechanism that opens the door. This works, but the person still gets hit by the door.

Some modern elevators solve this problem with light. A beam of light is sent across the doorway from one side of the door. A light detector on the other side of the doorway catches the light. As long as the beam is uninterrupted, an electrical circuit continues closing the door. If the beam of light is broken, the detector no longer receives light. This causes a switch to be thrown, and the circuit is broken. The door opens.

Automatic Conveyor Belts

Light is used in a similar way in supermarkets. A beam of light is sent across the conveyor belt near the cash register. On the other side of the belt there is a light detector. The light used is usually invisible infrared. When the conveyer brings an object to that point, the item blocks the beam of light from getting to the detector, and the belt stops. You can stop it yourself by putting your hand in front of the beam. (Ask for permission first.)

Fancy Door Ringers

In the olden days people used to hang bells on the doors of their stores. When the door opened, the bell rang, and the clerk knew that someone had entered. Today's high-tech world has updated the bell-ringing announcement of customers. Many stores (especially in malls) have doorbells that work by detecting light.

A beam of light is sent out across the doorway so that it strikes a reflecting object that looks like a bike reflector. The reflector bounces the light back to a detector near the light source. When you enter the store, you break that beam with your body. This causes a switch to be thrown, which closes an electric circuit that rings a bell. Try the next experiment to see a way to get by the doorbell without ringing it.

Fool a Doorbell

Materials & Equipment

- a flat bike reflector
- a store that has an automatic doorbell like the one described above

Procedure

Ask someone who works in the store if you can try this experiment before you do it. Look for the instrument that transmits the beam of light across the store door. It should be right across from the reflector that is mounted on the door frame. Without blocking any of the invisible beam with your body, put the bike reflector into the beam's path near the center of the doorway. Once you are holding the reflector in place, just walk through the door between it and the reflector that is mounted on the door frame. When you are through, lift the reflector up; the bell shouldn't ring.

Here's What's Happening

The bike reflector is made up of tiny *retroreflectors*. A retroreflector has many surfaces, each with a different angle. An ordinary flat mirror can reflect a beam back to its source, but it can do this only if it is held in exactly the right position. The many reflecting surfaces of all the retroreflectors make it possible to reflect some of

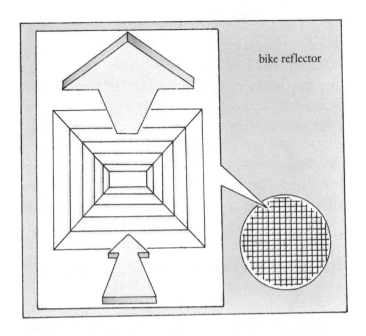

bike reflector

the incoming light back to the source without a perfect alignment. The instrument that transmits the light has a detector right next to it. When the light strikes the reflector on the door frame, it gets sent back to its source, where the detector is waiting for it. When you put the bike reflector in the path of the beam, it reflects the light back to the detector before it ever gets to the reflector on the door frame. As your body goes through the door, the beam is not broken, so the bell doesn't ring. Since the bike reflector is made up of retroreflectors, it doesn't matter if you tilt it slightly (something you might try), because some light will always get sent back to where it came from regardless of the angle of the light that hits the reflector.

Astronauts have put high-quality retroreflectors on the moon. Laser beams fired up to the moon can strike a retroreflector and return to earth, where they are detected. This allows scientists to measure accurately the time it takes light to make a round trip to the moon. Since we know how fast light travels, this kind of measurement allows us to compute the position of the moon at any given time.

PHOTOSYNTHESIS

Of all the amazing light-catching and light-transforming processes, none is more important than the effect of sunlight on green plants. The leaves of green plants are food factories. Carbon dioxide from the air combines with water in the leaf of a plant to form sugars. Building a sugar molecule is like climbing a hill: It takes energy. Plants get this energy from sunlight. The light-catching ingredient in a plant is the green pigment *chlorophyll*. The entire process is called *photosynthesis* which means "making with light."

The energy stored in sugar molecules is used for the complex chemical processes of all living things, which include the building of molecules of other necessary substances like proteins and fats. Green plants are at the bottom of the food chain, providing food for almost all other living things either directly or indirectly. Your body uses the energy in food for growth, heat production, motion, even thinking. Fossil fuels—oil, gas, and coal—are the ancient remains of once-living plants and animals. Energy from the sun, which was trapped and stored by green plants millions of years ago, is released as heat and light when the fuels are burned.

You can see for yourself the kind of light plants use for photosynthesis in the next experiment.

THE LIGHT THAT MAKES FOOD

In this experiment the presence of starch in a plant leaf demonstrates that photosynthesis has taken place. Starch is a large molecule made up of smaller sugar molecules. The formation of starch is one way food is stored in a plant. Starch can be tested for with iodine solution.

Materials & Equipment
- a healthy geranium plant
- aluminum foil
- scissors
- straight pins
- red, green, yellow, blue, and clear cellophane
- rubber bands or tape
- a stove (*Ask an adult for permission before you use the stove.*)

- a small pot of water
- tongs or a slotted spoon
- a small bowl and a larger bowl it will fit into
- rubbing alcohol *(Caution: Alcohol can be poisonous, and it is flammable. It should be kept away from your stove, or any other heat source, at all times.)*
- several white saucers
- iodine solution from a pharmacy, further diluted one part iodine to about ten parts water *(Caution: Iodine is poisonous, and it stains.)*

Procedure

Leave the geranium plant in a dark closet for at least twenty-four hours. Cut out identical foil shapes that are small enough to cover only part of a geranium leaf—say one-inch squares. Put a square on the top and bottom surface of a leaf so that they are over each other. Hold them in place with pins. Make a partially covered leaf for each color cellophane you have, plus one. Cut out squares of cellophane that are large enough to be gathered up into a loose bag over the leaf. (You need to leave plenty of air around each leaf.) Fasten the gathered cellophane around the stem with a rubber band or tape. Leave one partially blocked leaf uncovered or cover it with clear cellophane. Place the plant in sunlight for a day.

The next step is to test the leaves for starch. Be sure to keep track of which leaf received which

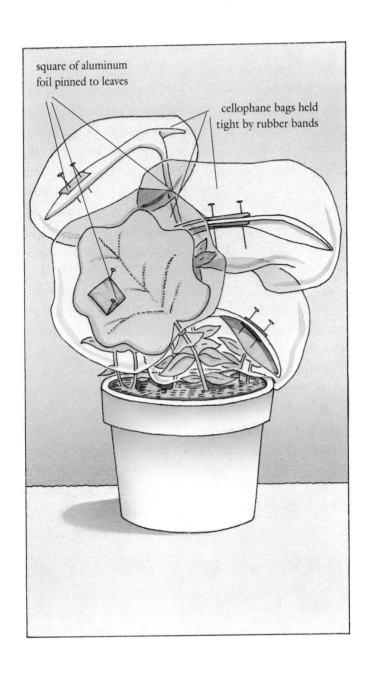

square of aluminum
foil pinned to leaves

cellophane bags held
tight by rubber bands

color light. Remove a leaf from the plant. Take off the foil and put the leaf in a pot of boiling water for one minute. This kills the leaf and softens the cell walls. Using tongs or a slotted spoon, put the leaf in a small bowl with rubbing alcohol and set the bowl in hot water in the larger bowl. *(Make sure that there are no flames around, and keep the alcohol away from the hot stove, as the alcohol is quite flammable.)* The chlorophyll in the leaf will dissolve into the alcohol, leaving the leaf white. Carefully spread the leaf out in a saucer and rinse it with cool water. Pour off the rinse water. Do the same for the other leaves with blocked spots, marking the colors. (You could put the cellophane for each leaf under its saucer as a way of keeping track.)

Pour diluted iodine solution over the leaf. The parts of the leaf that received the proper wavelengths of light will turn a blue-black color, indicating that photosynthesis has taken place and that starch has formed. The places that were shielded from the light will take on the brownish color of the iodine. (You can check out the color change by putting iodine on food items that you know contain starch, such as bread or pasta.)

Here's What's Happening

Chlorophyll is green because it absorbs the wavelengths of light in the red and blue-violet regions of the spectrum and reflects the green wavelengths. Sunlight, of course, has all wavelengths so your leaf that was in sunlight (covered with clear cellophane) will show the photosynthesis that occurred during your experiment. The leaf that was in green cellophane should show no starch formation. All the green light is reflected by the leaves, and the green cellophane let through only green light, but no red or blue-violet light. The leaf that was in red light should show some starch formation, since some of the wavelengths that are important for photosynthesis are present in red light. The same is true for blue and yellow.

LIGHT AND THE ENERGY CRISIS

The world's need for energy for running our factories and homes is constantly increasing. But the burning of fossil fuels is contaminating the environment and possibly is costing us our health. (They are also not renewable—oil and coal are being rapidly used up and cannot be replaced.) Scientists have been looking for many years for clean energy sources that are practical and inexpensive. Sunlight is certainly one of them.

We know how to capture the sun's rays and turn them into electricity using solar panels. We know how to heat water in homes by trapping heat from the sun with a solar heater that also uses solar panels. We have even made experimental solar-power plants by arraying many light reflectors over a large area. The reflectors trap sunlight and focus it to heat water, turning it into steam that runs turbines.

Solar energy is used to run spacecraft and has even powered some experimental automobiles that were lightweight, but that were slow compared to gas-burning cars. We have not yet developed a technology that makes solar energy cheap enough and efficient enough to be practical. Some promising new materials are being developed that may make it practical for homes in sunny parts of the world to be powered completely by solar panels. Harnessing the sun's rays will be part of the solution to the energy crisis.

INDEX

Page numbers of illustrations and diagrams appear in *italics*.

aberration, 74, 100
air (earth's atmosphere)
    composition of, 107
    index of refraction, 82, 84, 94
    sunlight in, 98, 100, *106*, 107
    why the sky is blue, 105, *106*,
      107
    why sunsets are orange, 105,
      106, 107
Alhazen, 2
arc lamps, 3
astigmatism, 74
    experiment on, 72–76, *73*, *75*
    in eye, 76
atmosphere. *See* air
automatic conveyor belts, 183

black-light bulb, 122–23
    See also fluorescence
bubbles, soap, 130, 138
    black spots on, 139, 140
    colors on, 139–40, *140*

cellulose, 20–21
chlorophyll, 186, 190
chromatic aberrations, 100
"circle of least confusion," 74
color
    black objects, 109
    in clear acetate, 141–42
    and constructive interference,
      139
    and diffraction, 130
    dominant, 113–14
    experiments on, 110–23, *111*,
      116
    fluorescent, 122–23

    and human eye, 109, 114, 177
    and interference, 130
    and laundry detergent, 121,
      122
    on oil slicks, 141
    and polarized light, 168, 170
    primary colors of light, 114
    in printing, 117, 118, 119–20
    shades, 114
    on soap bubbles, 139–40, *140*
    in stress birefringence, 165–66
    on television, 117–19
    and transparent materials,
      120–21
    unseen, 125, *126*, 127
    wheel, 115–17, *116*
    white objects, 109
    See also light
compact disc, *4*
    color on, 130, 145–46
    players, 3, 125
contact lenses, 46
critical angle, 82, *83*

da Vinci, Leonardo, 46
diamond
    index of refraction, 40
    sparkling of, 79
diffraction, 134, 144
    and blue sky, 105, *106*
    and compact discs, 130, 146
    and feather, 144–45
    grating, 145, 146
    and holograms, 147, *148*, *149*,
      150
    and ripple tank, 133–35, *135*,
      144

door bells, 183–86

eclipses
  lunar, 17–18, *17*
  solar, 18–19, *18*
Edison, Thomas, 3
electric eyes, 182–83
electricity
  battery, invention of, 174
  current, 174
electromagnetic spectrum, 125,
  126, 127
elevator door openers, 182
energy, 174
  chemical, 174
  electrical, 174
  heat as, 174, 175
  law of conservation of, 175
  light as, 173–75
  mechanical, 174
  and nerve, firing of, 177
  other forms of, 175
  solar, 175
eye, *179*
  afterimage, 175–77, *176*
  astigmatism, 76
  blindspot, 177–80, *178*, *179*
  cones, 177
  focusing in, 43, *45*, 76
  how we see color, 109, 114
  how we see objects, 63
  lens, 176, *179*
  optic nerve, 177, 179, *179*
  receptor cells, 1–2, 177
  retina, 43, *45*, 176–77, *179*,
    179–80
  rods, 177
  vision, light as basis of,
    175–80
  vision problems, 43, *45*, 76
eyeglasses, 43
  bifocal, 46
  first made, 44
  for farsightedness, 44, *45*
  for nearsightedness, 44, *45*, 46

spectacles, origin of word, 44

Faraday, Michael, 174
farsightedness, 43, 44, *45*
fax machines, 5
feather fringes, 144–45
fiber-optics
  cables, *4*, 5, 79–80, 86
  and total internal reflection,
    79, 84–85
  uses of, 79–80, 85–86
Fick, A. E., 46
fire, as light source, 3
fluorescence
  "Day–Glo" colors, 123
  lights, 3, 123
  materials, 122
focal point, 51
fossil fuel, 175, 187, 191
Franklin, Benjamin, 46
fringe patterns. *See* interference

Galileo, 26, 47
gamma rays, 125, *126*
gelatin, and transparency, *91*, 92
glare, 153, 156–57
glass
  and color, 120–21
  and fiber optics, 79–80
  green, 121
  index of refraction, 41, 82, 84
  for lenses, 121
  and total internal reflection,
    79–80, *83*
grocery scanners, 3, *4*, 125

heat
  and absorption of light,
    109–10
  and energy, 174–75
  and infrared light, 125
  and solar energy, 192
Hero, 2, 26
holograms, 5, 146–51
  on credit cards, 3, *4*, 5, 125,

150, 151
object beam, 147, *148*
reference beam, 147, 148, *148*
transmission, 147, *148*, *149*
two-image, 151
white-light, 147, 151

incandescent electrical light, 3, 123
index of refraction. *See* refraction
infrared light/radiation, 64, 125, *126*
interference
  bands or fringes, 136, 142, 147–48
  constructive, 139
  destructive, 140
  and holograms, 147–48, *148*
  moiré pattern, 143–44
  and oil slick, 130, 141
  and ripple tank, 130, 135–38, *137*
  and soap bubbles, 130, 138–41, *140*
invisible light, 64, 125, *126*, 127

Janssen, Zacharias, 47
Joule, James, 174

laser
  discovery of, 123–24
  and holograms, 147–51, *148*, *149*, *150*
  how it works, 124
  origin of name, 124
  uses of, 3, *4*, 125, 186
laundry detergent, 121–22
law of conservation of energy, 175
lens, *42*, 43
  aberrations in, 74
  astigmatism in, 74, *75*, 76
  bifocal, 46
  concave, 44, *45*

contact, 46
convex, 44, *45*, 50
  experiments using, 48–62, *49*, *50*, *52*, *53*, *54*, *55*, *59*
  in eye, 43
  in eyeglasses, 43–44, *45*, 46
  first made, 44
  glass for, 121
  grinding, 44, 46–47, 59–61
  ice, 57–61, *59*
  in microscope, 47
  origin of word, 44
  polarized, *152*, 153
  in telescope, 47
light
  and air temperature, 38
  ancient ideas about, 2, 26
  blue, 98, 105, *106*, 107, 113, 114–15, 168, 170, 190–91
  energy, 174–75, 191–92
  green, 113, 114–15, 190–91
  heat (or energy) and infrared, 109–10, 125, *126*, 174–75, 192
  mixing, 112–15
  and photochemistry, 181
  and photosynthesis, 186–91, *189*
  properties of, miscellaneous, 12, 25, 63–64, 173
  rays, 12–13, *14*, 19
  red, 97, 98, 100, 105, 107, 112, 113, 114–15, 170, 190–91
  slowing down, 28, 31, *32*, 33, 40, 82
  sources of, 3, 12, 146
  speed of, 25–28, 40
  technological uses of, 3, 5, 125, 191–92
  theories about, 2–3, 173–75
  ultraviolet, 122–23, 125, *126*
  violet, 97–98, 100
  white, 97, 109, 114
  yellow, 113, 114, 191

See also diffraction; interference; laser; lens; polarized light; reflection; refraction; shadows; total internal reflection (TIR); translucency; transparency
lightning, 25
Lippershey, Hans, 47
liquid crystal display (LCD), *162*, 163–64

magnifying glass, 50–51, *50*
Malpighi, Marcello, 47
Mayer, Julius, 174–75
Michelson, Albert, 27
micron, defined, *126*
microscope, 47
microwaves, 125, *126*
mirage, 37–38, *37*, *39*
mirror, 64, 184
    astigmatism in, 74, *75*, 76
    curved, 69
    See also reflection; retroreflectors
moiré patterns, 143–44
moon
    eclipse of, 17–18, *17*
    position of, measuring, 186
    retroreflectors on, 186
    shadow of, 18–19
Morley, Edward, 27

nearsightedness, 43, 44, *45,* 46
nerve, firing of, 177
Newton, Isaac, 97

object beam, 147, *148*
oil slicks, 141
opaque objects, 12, 21
    black, 109
    and color, 109, 120
    white, 109
opticians, 47, 59, 61
optics, science of, 3

paint thinner, index of refraction, 41
paper
    experiment to make translucent, 20–21
    oiled, 21
    tracing, 21–22
particle theory of light, 2, 19
penumbra. See shadows
photochemical reaction, 180–81
photocopiers, 5
photography, 181
photosynthesis, 186–91, *189*
pigments, mixing, 119–20
pixels, 118–19
polarized light
    and color, 168, 170
    depolarizing, 167
    experiments on, 153–70, *155,* *159, 161, 162, 169*
    flopping, 159–60, *162,* 163–64, 165, 166, 167–68, *169*, 170
    and liquid crystal displays (LCD), *162*, 163–64
    and rainbows, 160–61, *161*
    and stress birefringence, 165–66
Pope Leo X, 44, 46
printing, color in, 117, 118, 119–20
prism, 97
    making from water and mirror, 98–100, *99*
    and rainbows, 103, *104*
projector, making a, 54–56, *55*

radio
    telescope, 127
    waves, 125, *126*, 127
rainbow
    making a, 102–3, *104*
    making a, appear and disappear, 160–61, *161*
    in nature, 103, *104*

and polarized light, 161, *161*
Rayleigh, John W. S., 105
reference beam, 147, 148, *148*
reflection, 64
   and critical angle, 82, *83*
   diffuse, 68
   and electric eyes, 182–86
   experiments on, 64–76, *66,*
      70, 71, 73, 75, 184–86, *185*
   and mirrors, 64, *66*
   and normal line, 82
   retroreflector, 184–86, *185*
   specular, 67, 68
   total internal reflection (TIR),
      79–94, *81, 83, 85, 87, 89,*
      91, 93
   and vision, 63
   See also total internal reflec-
      tion (TIR)
refraction, 28
   and colored bands (chromatic
      aberrations), 100
   experiments on, 28–29, *30,*
      33–36, *34, 35,* 37–41, *37,*
      39, 48–62, *49, 50, 52, 53,*
      55, 59
   explained, 31, *32,* 33
   and eyeglasses, 43–44, *45,* 46
   index of, 40–41, 82, 84, 94
   and mirages, 37–38, *37, 39*
   and vision, 43–44, *45*
   See also lens
remote control (TV or VCR), 5,
   64
   bouncing signal off the wall,
      67–69
   using from another room,
      64–67, *66*
retroreflector, 184–86, *185*
ripple tank
   described, 129
   diffraction in, 133–35, *135*
   interference in, 135–38, *137*
   making a, 130–33, *131, 132*
Roemer, Olaus, 27

ROY G. BIV, 97

shadows, *8*
   activities for making, 14, *15,*
      16, 21–22
   experiments on, 10–11, *11,*
      12–14
   hunting for, 9
   penumbra, 11, *11,* 12, 13, 16,
      18, 102
   umbra, 11, *11,* 12–13, 16, 18
   variables, 14
   See also eclipses
silhouettes, 16
silver iodide, 181
sky, why it's blue, 105, *106,* 107
solar energy, 175, 191–92
sound, speed of, 25, 28
spectacles. *See* eyeglasses
spectrum, visible
   colors of, 97, 100, 109
   and diffraction grating, 145,
      146
   experiments on, 98–108, *99,*
      104, 106
   ROY G. BIV, 97
   separation of colors in, 100
   See also color; electromagnetic
      spectrum
speed of light. *See* light
starch, 187, 188, 190
stars
   analyzing light from, 145
   astigmatism and seeing, 76
stress birefringence, 165–66
sun
   eclipse of, 18–19, *18*
   as light source, 2
   See also solar energy; sunlight
sunglasses, polarized, 153
   experiments using, 156–70,
      157, 169
sunlight
   and air, 98, *106,* 107
   colors of, 97, 105, *106,* 107,

191
as energy source, 175, 191–92
and photosynthesis, 186–91,
189
ultraviolet in, 122
See also solar energy
sunset
making a, 103–5
in nature, 105, *106*, 107

telescope
discovery of, 47
radio, 127
television
big-screen, 71–72, 119
color for, 118–19
light from, *52*, 53–54, *55*
moiré patterns on, 144
projector, making a, 54–56, *55*
turning on from another
room, 64–67, *66*
watching with a mirror,
69–71, *70*, *71*
See also remote control (for TV
or VCR)
Thompson, Benjamin (Count
Rumford), 174
total internal reflection (TIR)
and critical angle, 82, *83*
and diamonds, 79
experiments on, 80–94, *81*,
83, *85*, *87*, *89*, *91*, *93*
and glass, 79
and normal line, 82
and water, 79
See also fiber optics
translucency, 19–20
experiments on, 20–22
of paper, 20
transparency, 19
and color, 120–21
and critical angle, 82, *83*
and gelatin, 90–92, *91*
and glass, 120–21
and index of refraction,

40–41, 82
and normal line, 82
and speed of light, 40, 82
transmitting light, 120

ultraviolet light, 122–23, 125,
126
umbra. *See* shadows

vision. *See* eye
von Helmholtz, Hermann, 175

water
colored lights in, 100–101
and index of refraction, 84, 94
prism from, 98–100, *99*
and total internal reflection,
79
See also wave
wave
crest, 31, 129
diffraction of, 130, 133–35,
135, 136, 144–45, 146,
147, *148*, *149*, *150*
interference of, 130, 135–44,
137, 147–51
and ripple tank, 129–38
theory of light, 2, 29, 31
trough, 31, 129
types of, 125, *126*, 127
vibration of light, 154, 156
water, 129–38
wavelength, 129
long, 125, *126*, 127, 170
as measure of color, 97–98,
105, 107, 168, 170, 191
short, 125, *126*, 168, 170
of ultraviolet light, 124, 125,
126

X rays, 125, *126*

Young, Thomas, 174